# A Battle for Destiny

## 55 Days of warfare and rest

Jervae Brooks

A Battle for Destiny

ISBN: 978-1-60920-006-0
Printed in the United States of America
©2010 by Jervae Brooks
@2013 Revision by Jervae Brooks
All rights reserved

Library of Congress Cataloging-in-Publication Data

Cover and interior design by Ajoyin Publishing, Inc.
Back cover photo by Ashley Paul.


Ajoyin Publishing, Inc.
P.O. 342
Three Rivers, MI 49093
www.ajoyin.com

Please direct your inquiries to admin@ajoyin.com

# A Battle for Destiny

*55 Days of warfare and rest*

*Jervae Brooks*

Ajoyin Publishing
P.O. Box 342 Three Rivers, MI 49093
888.273.4JOY
www.ajoyin.com

# Endorsements

"To learn the message of God's encompassing peace and rest in the midst of great physical suffering is as much of a miracle as God's healing of the physical body. This book will take you on a journey that will encourage your faith."

Jane Hansen Hoyt
President/CEO of Aglow International

"Jervae Brooks has done a masterful job in writing, A Battle for Destiny. It is a true story about the amazing faithfulness of God to a husband and wife in the middle of their fight to see Dwight's destiny fulfilled. Being Jervae's and Dwight's pastor has helped me see them live through the story you are about to read. It will bless you and challenge you in the fight for your own destiny. It is full of nuggets of truth lived in the arena of real life trial and adventure. This is literally a fight for the physical life of Dwight. It was the fight of a life for Jervae as well. God has a destiny for you! May this book help you reach it for the glory of God."

Dan C. Hammer, Senior Pastor
Sonrise Chapel - Everett, Washington

"We may safely assume that God desires the best for us and that only He knows what that would be. However, we are not to remain passive in the midst of discomfort, disease and pain. The 55 days of problems, and the love that believes a promise, is a declaration that LOVE WINS! and knowing that love never fails.

*Jervae is a spiritual warrior who fought a fight and won. The life lesson is don't give up! He will either give us what we ask for or something better. Dwight and Jervae received both. We exchange our weakness for His power. Although the world is full of suffering, theirs is a testimony of overcoming."*

Leif Hetland

President - Global Mission Awareness

# Contents

# Dedication

**This book is dedicated to my sister**

*Susan Kay Miller*
*August 3, 1952 – September 28, 2009*

*You fought the good fight,*
*you finished the race,*
*and you remained faithful.*
                    *II Timothy 4:7*

# Thank You

*T*o my husband for his determination to never give up, and to live his life with integrity before God. I love you completely.

To our daughter Terry, and grandchildren Crystal, Christen and Christopher, for believing in God's promises and loving us so much. Racquel, Jessica, Megan, Austin and Kayla—thank you for praying for your Grandpa!

To our church family—Pastor Dan Hammer, Pastor Doug Martin, Scott and Kay Rice, Bob and Cheney McGowan, John and Michelle Iwanczuk and all the dear friends at Sonrise Chapel in Everett, Washington. Too many to name! You understood the warfare and spent countless hours in prayer battling for us.

To my sisters and brothers in Aglow—Jane Hansen Hoyt, all those on the Leadership Team at Aglow headquarters, Martha Stanley, Joyce Jones Moss, Aglow leaders and friends around the world. There are no greater warriors I would rather go to battle with.

**Special thanks to** Martha Stanley, Kay Rice, and Rob Bingaman for your willingness to read these pages over and over. Your editing suggestions were excellent and greatly appreciated.

About two weeks into our stay in ICU my friend, Kay Rice, gave me a copy of T.D. Jake's devotional, *Hope for Every Moment—365 Inspirational Thoughts for Every Day of the Year*. Each page is not dated with the month and day, but instead each one is simply titled Day 1, Day 2, etc. One day, between times of suctioning the saliva out of Dwight's mouth when he began to choke, I decided to compare Day 1 in this devotional with my notes of what had taken place that day. I was amazed to read, day after day, scriptures and devotional thoughts that mirrored what had happened—or what I needed to hear for that day. This went on for the entire 55 days. After that the devotionals no longer "fit" each of our days in the same way. Those devotionals had given me hope, and knowledge that God was with me. It was as though T.D. Jakes had written this just for me. Thank you Bishop Jakes!

# Foreword from Dwight

At the time of this writing my wife, Jervae, and I have been married for nearly 40 years and, like most couples who have been married that long, have gone through many life experiences together. Some were joys that allowed us a clear view from the top of the mountain, and some were sorrows that took us deep into the valley. Thankfully, we've gone through them together. And together we have learned that the experiences in the valley are where God teaches us the greatest lessons.

One night back in May of 1976 God met us both, quite unexpectedly, and life has never been the same since. That night I committed my life back to God as I had known Him in my youth, and miraculously was no longer an angry young man running away. Instead I began the new journey of a man who wanted to love my wife and family and to be used by God. Jervae's life and our marriage changed that night too, and we are both so grateful for God's love and power to save and restore.

This is actually our story, but I can't be the one to write it. I was there physically, but I have little memory of most of this journey. Of the 55 days I spent in the intensive care unit I remember parts of only 5 or 6 days. In those moments of awareness I felt determined to never give up and I am thankful to God for being my strength.

A short while before all of this happened I felt the Lord speak something to my spirit that was very clear. I believe God was prophetically speaking to me but, as we too often do, I did not fully understand what He was telling me.

One day sometime during August 2008, the month before this whole adventure began, I heard God's still small voice speak to my spirit. He told me He was going to teach me about "Spiritual Warfare." When we hear such a thing from God we hope He will allow us to learn not first-hand, but from other people's experiences! Those were my thoughts anyway. At that time I was enrolled in the Wagner Leadership Institute in our church (I still am) and in the course of our studies had read many books, including some on spiritual warfare. So it didn't seem so unusual to hear God speak this to me. Little did I know that I was soon going to be thrown into the most significant battle of my life.

Dwight Brooks
May 2009

# Foreword from Jervae

Many who know us and walked through this journey with us have encouraged me to write this book. I wanted to share about the things that took place during these incredible days, but struggled with how to go about such a project. One day I was praying about writing "my" book, and told God that I didn't have the gift of talking and thinking all the thoughts and ideas like one needs to write a book.

Often as I'm enjoying reading a story or teaching I marvel at all the wonderful ways the author thinks to elaborate on a subject. I often feel like Moses when he pleaded with God to find someone else to talk because he could not speak without stammering. The words of this prayer were barely off my lips when I heard Him speak to my heart. He said, "It isn't your words I want you to write. You write the words I want you to write. I want you to tell what I did."

Well, that put a whole new light on why this needs to be written. I pray that as you read in the pages of this book about what God did for ordinary people like Dwight and me, that you will be filled with hope and the faith to believe that He will work in miraculous ways in your circumstance too. My prayer is that this will be much more than a testimony. I pray that in these pages you will come to know my God; the One who is the wonderful and safe place I run to and where I find all my strength to face whatever the day might hold.

Jervae Brooks
May 2009

# Part I

# *The Journey Begins*

*T*his story actually begins back in November, 1988. Dwight had suddenly developed a terrible pain in his abdomen. He was in the hospital for 20 days in desperate pain but none of the extensive tests the doctors performed showed any cause, nor any assurance that surgery could fix it. Throughout that month of November, every day after getting our youngest of three daughters off to school, I would go to the hospital usually staying until about 10:00 at night. Every day or so there was a new diagnosis. Everything from pancreatic cancer to heart disease was suspected. He saw every specialist except maternity! He had no bowel tones, meaning his digestive system was not working.

At that time I didn't know about the supernatural "rest" that God wants to give to us, even in the midst of stressful circumstances. So, many times during those days I was gripped by fear. Panic nearly overtook me at times when I could see my husband slipping toward death and not even our capable doctors knew what to do about it.

Every night when I went home I fell exhausted on my knees beside the bed and pleaded with God to spare Dwight's life. I believed in prayer but did not understand the power that was available to me through actually doing battle in the Holy Spirit—what I know now to be spiritual warfare.

Finally one morning after nearly three weeks in the hospital I walked past the nurses' station on the way to his room and saw all of his belongings on a small rolling cart. I thought to myself, "He has died!" When I got to his room I saw he was still alive, but barely. The nurses were preparing to move him to ICU, and he would be having exploratory surgery as soon as they could prepare him. He was dying. They couldn't wait any longer.

He was very weak and his oxygen was turned so high it was noisy in the room. I had to put my ear right up to the oxygen mask to hear what he was trying to say to me. He was incoherent but trying to talk.

Finally the doctor came into the room, and began to explain the dangers of surgery. It seemed redundant to explain that "he could die" at that point, but I knew they had to go through those formalities. In the midst of the doctor's explanation, suddenly Dwight sat up in bed. A moment earlier he had no strength to even speak! He sat up in bed and witnessed to the doctor in a strong enough voice he could be heard throughout the room.

"Doctor, I'm not afraid to die. I believe in Jesus Christ. I believe in hospitals too. That's why I'm here. But I'm not afraid to die!" Then he slumped back on his pillow.

I was shocked. The doctor was stunned, stammered

through the rest of his comments, and left the room. Weeks later Dwight wept as I told him what he had said. He didn't remember any part of that day, but he wept with gratitude to God that what was in his spirit at that moment, so close to death, was Jesus.

They took him to surgery. I went to the phone and called everyone I knew to start praying. My faith had risen as I heard Dwight testify to the doctor, and my fear turned into action. This time we knew what to pray for… a successful surgery, the source of the problem to be found, and life for my husband.

The surgery was successful, but what the doctors found was shocking. Gangrene was in his intestines. Tiny blood clots would later be found in his intestines that had grown slowly over the weeks cutting off circulation. The surgeon removed the infected section. When I saw Dwight back in his ICU room, he was unconscious and on total life support. Dwight's system was poisoned from the gangrene, and that was threatening his life.

That evening when the doctor came to talk to me about Dwight's condition, he explained each of the numbers on the monitor, where they were, and where they needed to be. There were about five major bodily functions that needed to come into balance in order for him to live through the night. It all sounded overwhelming.

When the doctor finished explaining all this to me I said, "Doctor that doesn't sound possible." He looked me straight in the eye and said, "It's not possible."

But God had other plans.

He lived through the night. Then he lived through

the next day, and then the next night. And it went like that for a number of days until he was finally released from ICU. It was another month before he was released from the hospital to come home, and during that month he developed blood clots in his legs, cysts in his abdomen, and pneumonia.

When he finally came home, on his birthday—December 16—he still was very weak and very sick. But he had talked his doctor into letting him come home on his birthday. Our daughters had made a big sign "Welcome home Dad." When he got into the living room and sat in his chair we wept. Later that night, as I laid in bed next to him listening to his chest rattle with pneumonia I prayed, "God, please help me know how to take care of him now."

It was a long journey back to strength but Dwight is a strong and determined man. He was not going to let this rob him of his life. He loved to hunt and to fish, and he loved to work. He resumed his life more quickly than anyone expected. But there were also many appointments with doctors trying to figure out why all this had happened.

It took about two years of various consultations and tests. Finally, he was diagnosed with what is now called Protein C deficiency. In 1990 there was no name as yet for this condition and they called it "thrombo-modulyn deficiency." Dwight was told he was the fifth person in the United States to be diagnosed with this disorder. It is a blood disorder that causes the blood to clot, and the treatment is blood thinning medication.

That sounds pretty straightforward, but back when Dwight was on life support all of his major organs had quit working at different times, and in one of those times a large blood clot formed in the portal vein through his liver. Over those couple years the increased blood pressure in the smaller veins caused varicose veins to form in his esophagus and stomach, making him a high bleeding risk. Anyone with this condition should <u>never</u> take any type of blood thinning medication. But to treat the Protein C deficiency, his blood had to be thinned. So he walked a fine line between the high risk of internal bleeding, and the possibility of developing blood clots somewhere in his body.

I've thought many times of the phrases, "Live each day like it could be your last," and even "Eat, drink and be merry, for tomorrow you may die." Those aren't scriptures, although they are often spoken like quotes from the Bible! But in Ecclesiastes 9:2 Solomon laments, "The same destiny ultimately awaits everyone…" meaning that we all will die some day. Dwight and I had to learn how to live like that. Love, serve God, leave nothing unsaid. Tomorrow may be too late.

## Part II

# Warfare

*F*ast forward to September 12, 2008.

A normal Friday morning at the office changed suddenly when my cell phone rang. I smiled as I saw my husband's picture on the caller ID. But as soon as I heard his voice I knew something was terribly wrong. Our lives would not be "normal" again for a very long time.

I heard an anguished moan, or maybe it was a scream. I can't even describe it. He said, "I'm throwing up blood!" I knew instantly that what the doctors had been saying was a possibility for the past 18 years had suddenly happened. I understood all too well what was taking place. Dwight was hemorrhaging from varicose veins in his esophagus, and because he also took blood thinning medication, I knew he could bleed to death very quickly.

"Where are you?" I said.

"I'm behind a store by my truck!" (He was at work, making a delivery.)

"Is there anyone around?"

"No, I'm all alone. I've called the plant and they called 911!"

"How far is it to the front of the store?"

"Too far, I can't make it!"

"You have to! Start walking! How far are you now?"

"My arm is going numb!"

"Don't stop! Keep on walking!"

By this time the women I work with at the head-quarters of Aglow International had heard my frantic phone conversation and gathered around the door of my office. They, too, knew what was happening because they had prayed for my husband many times over the years. I made eye contact with them as I paced the floor of my office and struggled to stay focused, not to scream out in panic myself, and to keep Dwight talking on the phone. I was compelling him with all the strength in me to fight for life!

My co-workers gathered for prayer in the meeting room of our office and began to fight in prayer with me even while I was still on the cell phone with Dwight. The war that would continue raging for the next 55 days had begun.

Looking back at that moment I believe God filled me with a measure of faith-filled determination that I had not had before. Years of hearing great messages and teachings had filled my head with knowledge of what God had spoken to other people. But here I was suddenly facing a life or death situation and there was no time to wonder what I needed to do. I began that moment fighting an unseen battle in the spiritual realm. Even though there was a definite medical explanation for what was happening in Dwight's body, somehow I "knew" in my spirit that I had to be a defender and not a victim.

After what seemed an eternity Dwight finally told me he had reached the front door of the store. I heard the voice of a woman helping him lie down on the floor. Then I heard sirens and suddenly a medic was on the phone asking my husband's name, birth date and to which hospital I wanted them to take him.

My Aglow sisters were in battle mode with me and didn't ask the questions they knew I couldn't answer. They prayed with me before we left the office, and my co-worker, Martha, drove me to the hospital. All the way to the downtown Seattle hospital we prayed, declared God's Word, and believed.

We declared that Dwight would live and not die. We prayed for strength and that God would surround Dwight and all the people at the hospital who were tending to him. We declared that God's healing power would surround him. We declared that we would believe not just what we saw with our eyes but what we knew in our spirits to be true—that God is all powerful and He died to heal our diseases.

I felt fear trying to overtake me. It wasn't the first time I had ridden to the hospital fighting fear and praying everything would be all right. It reminded me of one July night in 1992. We had a phone call from the hospital that our youngest daughter had been in a car accident and we should come right away. I was nearly paralyzed by fear that night and my legs felt as if they were wooden pegs as we ran from the car to the emergency room entrance.

Our youngest daughter, Tracy, had just turned 18, graduated from high school, and was ready to begin studying Theater in community college. She had become a beautiful young woman who wanted to be an actress who glorified God with her acting. After three days in the trauma unit we had to turn off her life support. Her body wasn't even bruised. But her neck was broken. God in His love allowed me to "see" the wings of the angels that were hovering to bring her to heaven, and I even felt the wind of their wings on my skin. From that day to this, the memory is very real and it comforts me.

I can't tell that long story here. It was a time of wrenching pain as if my own body, my very soul, was bloodied and torn. For years I felt myself clinging to what at times felt like remnants of faith. But with God as my ever-present anchor of sanity and amazing love, hope returned. Eventually even joy found its way back into my life. I praise God for His loving arms around me during those difficult years.

Here I was again, on my way to an emergency room not knowing how the day would end and praying with all the courage within me that I would not lose my husband as I had lost my daughter.

As Martha and I proclaimed God's promises and declared what I knew in my spirit was God's ultimate victory for Dwight—fear was replaced by a determination to do real battle in prayer.

Amazingly, it was only the day before that we had consulted with a renowned vascular surgeon, Dr. Kai Johannsen, at Swedish Medical Center in Seattle. Dwight had experienced some bleeding issues a month or so before and the gastroenterologist who treated him felt it was time to consult with a vascular surgeon about the possibility of some type of surgery to correct the internal problems he had dealt with for so many years. He made the appointment for Dwight with the same doctor who told us 18 years earlier that there was nothing more he could do for him. We hoped that medical advances over the years had changed that.

# Day 1

> *And, behold, there was a woman who had a spirit of infirmity eighteen years, and was bent over and could in no way lift herself up...He called her to Him, and said to her, Woman, you are loosed from your infirmity.*
> *Luke 13:11-12*

### From my journal

The healing journey of Dwight's infirmity of 18 years began today! God spared his life this night. Dr. told me not everyone lives through this type of situation.

*W*hen I arrived in the emergency room Dwight smiled through a blood-caked mustache and beard when he saw me. We looked at each other with eyes of understanding; not needing many words to know exactly what the other was thinking and feeling. So many times over the past 18 years we had been forced to talk about the possibility of this type of thing happening. But nothing prepares you for the reality of such a traumatic moment. I knew exactly what was happening, and how quickly he could bleed to death. The first of many units of blood had already been ordered for him and even before he was moved out of the emergency room into ICU (Intensive Care Unit) he filled another nausea bag with blood that he could not afford to lose.

When this happened he looked at me and said, "This will not take me out!" Together we allowed our faith to rise and believed God to carry him through this to a good end. This positive confession put us both in alignment to rest in the sovereignty of God. That kind of "rest" is every bit as proactive as doing battle with sword and shield!

In Part Three of this book I share more fully what God has shown me about His amazing gift of rest.

Our pastor, Dan Hammer, and a missionary friend who had just arrived from India, Pastor Matthew Thomas, came to the hospital en route from the airport. They arrived just as Dwight was being wheeled out of the emergency room and followed us up to the ICU floor. The doctors and nurses were working frantically to stabilize Dwight but they allowed these two godly men to come in and pray for him in those first moments of what would become a very long time in ICU. It was a holy moment as a hush fell in the room and the Holy Spirit was invited to comfort, to heal, and to sustain life. One of the nurses also laid hands on Dwight and added her prayers to theirs.

The hours that followed are a blur of many units of blood or plasma flowing into Dwight's arm, and of bed pans full of the same bright red blood. The nurses allowed me to stay in the room. They saw I remained calm as I immersed myself into what had to be done. I truly don't know how I was able to do that—except that my sprit was resting and believing in God's sovereignty as I fought physically and in prayer for my husband's life.

Dwight and I didn't talk much. All our attention was given to hanging on to life. When Dwight did talk, he proclaimed determination to never give up, and to fight a battle worthy to give glory to God.

Throughout the night I attended Dwight as the nurses were able to allow me to do so, or I paced the hallway and waiting room praying, declaring scripture and proclaiming God's promises over my husband. A few months earlier we had attended a conference at our church, Sonrise Chapel, and each of the attendees received a prophetic prayer which was recorded on tape. These prayers were spoken over each of us by mature Christian leaders who could discern spiritually, what God was saying to us. Prophecies like these are not to tell the future, or to tell a person what to do. Instead they are the way God gives encouragement and confirmation to something He has likely already been speaking to that person, quietly in their heart.

Dwight's word spoke strongly of his destiny. I knew his destiny had not yet been fulfilled! Hour after hour through the night I reminded God of that fact, and demanded that the enemy of his soul, who is Satan, be rendered powerless in his fight to steal the word of Jesus Christ from us.

In John 10:10 the Bible says that Satan came to earth to kill, steal and destroy. So that makes him my enemy because I knew he would try to steal the destiny God had for Dwight. A mighty strength rose up in me and I knew

I had to fight in prayer to protect what was ours from being stolen!

God gave me power to intercede in prayer through the Holy Spirit that night. I believe God gave me a gift of intercession and I was able to pray more boldly than I ever had before. I even reminded God that there were still prayers that God needed Dwight to pray on this earth! As I paced around the waiting room throughout that night, speaking loudly to God and pointing my finger in the air for emphasis I thought "Where did that come from? Is it okay to talk to God like that?" Yes, it is.

I'm reminded of how Moses interceded for the Israelites. The Bible tells us an amazing story in Numbers 14 of God's wrath burning against the people because of their constant rejection of Him. God told Moses He would destroy all the people and build of Moses a new nation far greater than they. But Moses interceded for the people before God and asked that He pardon their sins because of His magnificent, unfailing love. Moses reminded God of all the miracles the Egyptians had witnessed when God brought the Israelites out of Egypt and across the Red Sea, and what would they think now if the same God of the Israelites killed them all?

In the previous months God had begun using Dwight in some pretty dramatic ways as he prayed for people during the prayer times in our church. Also, the church men's group was growing under Dwight's leadership. Exciting things were happening there too. People were watching this man change and grow in the Lord before their eyes. I passionately reminded God that Dwight still had things to do on this earth. Things that God had begun in him and, as Moses reminded God, what would people think if his life ended now?

I know this came from the Holy Spirit and my God did honor that prayer. I've thought of that at times this past year when I've ministered alongside Dwight and listened to his prayer for someone and the Lord healed them in their body or their emotions. We all are God's hands, feet and mouthpieces on this earth, and He did need Dwight to pray that prayer out loud for Him.

Have you ever asked God, "What prayers do You need me to pray for You?" That puts a new light on our prayer life, doesn't it?

About midnight the decision was made to sedate and intubate Dwight (insert a breathing tube.) He had been given 9 units of blood during the past 12 hours and the doctors knew they had to stop the hemorrhaging to save his life. I was relieved that the sedation eased his suffering, but it also made me feel that he was so far away.

# Day 2

> "...the blood of Jesus Christ His Son cleanses us..."
> 1John 1:7

### From my journal

Yesterday & today D. rec'd 9 units of blood. Had to be intubated to stop the loss of blood—D. was put into a state of total dependence. His last words were "I'm determined. I'm going to be fine. Pray for me."

Between midnight and 7:00AM he did not have any more bleeding episodes. The sun was shining in the windows of his room and in the light of day I could see telltale signs of the massive and frequent blood loss of the night before. Dwight was lying quietly, sedated, and connected to the breathing machine.

The attending gastroenterologist was so kind and touched my shoulder as he said, "That was pretty tough, wasn't it." Then the tears I had held back all night came, as I allowed myself to be comforted. The doctor gently told me, "Your husband was very sick last night. Some people don't pull out of that kind of situation." I knew it had been very serious, but to hear a doctor admit that made it a little too real.

So God had spared his life that night. I asked if putting

in the breathing tube had relaxed his system and made the bleeding stop. The doctor said it was more a combination of all the things they had done, and were continuing to do…banding the varicose veins that were bleeding, the various medications and IV's. "And prayer," I added. The doctor agreed, "Yes, and prayer."

That day I felt impressed to read Psalm 71 in my New King James Bible. Courage filled me as I read these words that seemed to be written especially for Dwight. From the very first line, "*In You O Lord, I put my trust,*" the words comforted me and told me that God had more for my husband to accomplish this side of heaven. Verse 7 reads, "*I have become as a wonder to many, But you are my strong refuge.*" Dwight has confounded many doctors in his lifetime, as well as friends and family who have watched him turn from an angry young man, to a gentle and loving father walking strongly with God. And, "*You, who have shown me great and severe troubles, shall revive me again.*" Yes—God would revive Dwight again.

Another verse of this Psalm, verse 18, also told me that God was not yet ready to take my husband home with Him. "*…O God, do not forsake me, until I declare Your strength to this generation…*" Dwight has a special calling in his heart to reach out to young men who are trying to be good husbands and fathers but didn't have a father in their own lives to train them up in these Godly ways. His destiny was not yet fulfilled. I knew it was not the right time for the end of his days to come now. I was determined to storm heaven and secure the gates against hell to fight for my husband's life.

That day is so clear in my memory, and as I remember my sense of calm, I am still amazed. There is a resting in God that brings peace to the soul. It's true I didn't yet know all that would happen in the coming weeks—thank God He doesn't always tell us everything! But as I read that Psalm, and was also led to read Psalm 27, a divine security settled on the inside of me. A security so real that it gave me the assurance that God was fully in control.

It was as if the words of Psalm 27 became living and so tangible that I actually saw myself running to hide in His pavilion (verse 5). He set me high upon a rock (verse 5) and from that vantage point I could see His face. When He told me to seek His face (verse 8), with my whole heart I responded "Your face Lord, I will seek." He led me on a smooth path (verse 11) because of my enemies. The enemy of our soul, who is Satan, was attacking us with fear and hopelessness, trying to kill Dwight's body and my faith. And I truly "would have lost heart unless I had believed that I would see the goodness of the Lord in the land of the living." (verse 13.) He gave me courage to wait upon Him and to be of good courage, and He truly did strengthen my heart (verse 14).

Countless times in the following weeks—hundreds at least—I ran to hide and to rest in the shelter that God provided for me. That is the kind of God we serve; radiating power and authority, ready to do battle for us with sword drawn! Always available, He is waiting with open arms to hide us in the shelter of His love. Allowing us to rest because His greatness is taking care of everything.

# Day 3

> "To everything there is a season, a time for every purpose under heaven."
>
> Ecclesiastes 3:1

**From my journal**

Removed breathing tube. Terrible struggle & suffering. Dwight's 1st words to me were about Paul's struggles. With great determination D said, "how many times did Paul get 39 lashes? 5 times! And how many times was Paul beaten & each time thanked God for the privilege of suffering for Him!

Thirty-six hours later they removed the breathing tube, which in itself is a painful and frightening experience. I was asked to stand outside his room, and I listened and prayed as I heard the awful sounds through the curtain. I cringed as I heard him gag and cough, and prayed God would relieve his suffering.

As soon as I could, I went to his side. Dwight seemed fierce in his determination. His first words to me were, "How many times did Paul suffer 39 lashes?!"

I wasn't prepared for his question and, great woman of the Word that I am, responded, "Uh, umm, well I think…"

He interrupted me, "Five times! And how many times did he suffer for the sake of Christ and thank God for the privilege?!"

As I've said before, we both knew this was a battle in the spiritual realm, and it was a real fight for life. If determination alone was required, we felt up for it and determined to glorify God. I hope that statement doesn't sound lofty or super spiritual. Really, a shift into closer alignment seemed to have happened in our hearts and we recognized that we had received an assignment that we were determined to complete. We both felt rest in our souls, but were battling in our spirits.

# Day 6

> For the vision is yet for an appointed time.
>
> Habakkuk 2:3a

**From my journal**

This verse is in D's prophetic word from June. Today surgery was set—then postponed. It was not yet God's appointed day!

After that initial battle, the next few days were almost peaceful. The bleeding had stopped, his blood pressure was stabilized, and the decision was made to remove Dwight's spleen to lower blood pressure on the varicose veins in his stomach. We finally had time to talk. The surgery was postponed twice, which was a little stressful, but when we learned that the surgeon had been awake all night doing emergency surgeries and that he had postponed so he could be well rested for Dwight's surgery, we agreed that was a wise decision!

Normally people don't remain in ICU after they've stabilized, but given Dwight's precarious situation they did not want to move him from ICU in case he took a sudden turn for the worse. The nurses who had attended Dwight that first night were happy to see him sitting up in bed and chatting comfortably.

During one of those days while we were waiting for surgery, Dwight's good friend, Scott, was visiting, and he and Dwight were discussing some scriptures. Suddenly the curtains at the door of the hospital room opened and a tall young man asked if he could come in. He was the hospital chaplain assigned to ICU. Chaplain Robert, as I came to know him, entered the room, then stopped and looked surprised. He had "felt" the Spirit of God as he stepped into the room and was happy to pull up a chair. The three men began to share easily with each other. I stood at the foot of the bed feeling that it was a special time for them, and I was not surprised when Dwight told Chaplain Robert that he had a Word from God for him. Dwight asked if he could pray for him. It was a special moment, which began a very comforting friendship. Chaplain Robert stopped in each day after that.

# Day 9

> *I am God, and there is none like Me, declaring the end from the beginning, and from ancient times the things that are not yet done, saying, My counsel shall stand, and I will do all My pleasure.*
>
> *Isaiah 46:9b-10*

### From my journal

Our conversations of yesterday and today were: earned authority, the weight of glory, never give up, determination, we are heirs of the righteousness of God & our children are heirs to what we'll leave them with spiritually.

What do a husband and wife talk about in moments like those? What subjects seem important during an experience of traumatic and life threatening drama, and surgery which would be extremely risky for someone with Dwight's unusual health issues?

Some of our conversations revolved around my making phone calls for him to finalize the men's retreat that was to take place the next weekend. Dwight is the head of the men's ministry at our church, and all those last-minute arrangements had to be made. He finalized the plans from his hospital bed in ICU, all the men rallied and they had a wonderful retreat. What a blessing to receive a rambunctious phone call on speaker phone from all the guys at the retreat wishing him well!

Other conversations took on a serious tone. It seemed that thoughts of the kingdom of God filled Dwight's soul. I believe he was in sight of death's door even then.

We talked about earned authority. About how, when you have purchased something, it's yours. It belongs to you. And when you have walked through something, purchased it with suffering, you have purchased the authority to proclaim victory over it. Just as when Christ suffered for us on the cross and then rose again, He purchased the authority to proclaim victory over death. Christ carries us through times of suffering, and through our testimony He is glorified as we proclaim victory over that for which He has already paid the price.

*"Father, the hour has come. Glorify Your Son, that Your Son may glorify You, as You have given Him authority over all flesh, that He should give eternal life to as many as You have given Him"* (John 17:1a-2).

Jesus' prayers to the Father in John 17 are powerful, and speak of the authority He purchased through His suffering. He did this for us, that followers of Jesus Christ *"may be one as We are" (*John 17:11b*).*

We also talked about never giving up. Dwight himself had been in the Navy during the Vietnam War, but he talked for a long time about the men and women who are part of elite forces in the Armed Services. It is physically challenging, and the training is very painful. Men who are training to be Navy Seals endure daily rigorous training that leaves them in physical agony. Every day they feel tempted to quit. They know, when they lay down in their bunk at the end of each day of training that has left them with every muscle screaming and with feeling they cannot go on, all they would have to do is walk out into the yard and ring the bell and they could go home. No questions asked. They know that tomorrow will be just like today was, and tomorrow they'll want to quit again. But they also know that if they stay the course, if they do not give up, the prize at the end is being able to hold their heads high knowing they have remained steadfast. They have earned the right to be called a Navy Seal.

Dwight was helping me understand that he would not "ring the bell."

What if Jesus—in the midst of the scourging, the beating, the humiliation—had said, "Wait. Stop. You win. I'm not the Son of God!" What if He had given up?

We talked about the faith of Abraham. Even though he was a flawed man, his faith was great and Isaac became heir to the righteousness of his father as long as he followed in Abraham's footsteps. We read in Hebrews 11:

*"By faith Abraham obeyed when he was called to go out to the place which he would receive as an inheritance. And he went out, not knowing where he was going* (vs 8)... *Therefore from one man, and him as good as dead, were born as many as the stars of the sky in multitude—innumerable as the sand which is by the seashore.* (vs 12)*"*

And in Galatians 4:7

*"Therefore you are no longer a slave but a son, and if a*

*son, then an heir of God through Christ.*"

We were arming ourselves for battle.

In (T.D. Jakes') devotional, the scripture for Day 10 was, "*I shall not die, but live, and declare the works of the Lord* (Psalm 118:17).

Throughout these conversations I felt almost like an onlooker, going through the motions. Now, sitting with Dwight in his hospital room and listening to him "preach" to me all these things that were in his heart, seemed surreal. I just listened and wrote notes about the things he was saying. He just seemed to be speaking out the stirrings that God had put inside of him, and I could only contribute by capturing his thoughts on paper. Now as I write this I wonder about my actions, but at the time journaling was the only thing that seemed normal.

# Day 11

> O God, do not for-
> sake me, until I declare
> Your strength to this
> generation...
> Psalm 71:18b

**From my journal**

This is what D is called to.
It is his destiny. Today was
surgery. There will be a journey
to healing but the result will
be a return to the ministering
& praying for people that D
loves so much to do.

The morning of surgery Chaplain Robert came to pray with us. It was a sweet and peaceful time. We knew the risks, but also knew what God had promised. I felt like both of us were marching together into a battle, and I felt faith rise up in me that we would win.

I was told the surgery to remove Dwight's spleen would take three to six hours, then another one to two hours in the recovery room. I settled myself into the family surgical waiting room and made some phone calls to let our family and friends know the surgery was beginning. We surely wanted full prayer coverage at that time! I knew that the loved ones I called would each call many others—so the chain of prayer would be strong, and long!

I received a message from the operating room after

about two hours telling me the first part of the surgery had gone well and they were then beginning the spleen-ectomy. The surgeon came out and talked with me about two hours later. The whole thing had taken only four hours. That seemed to me a good sign!

The doctor said the surgery went well, although he was not able to do all that he had hoped. He explained everything he did, even drawing for me a picture of strange shapes and lines to explain why he had made the decisions he did during the surgery. He explained how he had hoped to accomplish a better solution for Dwight's long term health, but that doing any more would have put too great a strain on Dwight's system. During surgery they gave him several units of blood, and also re-circulated 600cc's of his own blood back into his system. The removal of Dwight's spleen would significantly reduce the blood pressure in his stomach, but it was not possible to insert a shunt which would have reduced the blood pressure in his esophagus. The doctor said he should be intubated (on the breathing machine) until the next day and out of the hospital in three days, "or until we're comfortable with him going home."

Again I felt calm, and now I sometimes wonder about that. Was I really "out of touch" with my emotions? No, I don't think so. I felt so confident in God and in what He had already spoken to my heart that I was able to honestly rest in that knowledge. The Jesus I know cares for me, and for my husband, so lovingly. He was allowing me to hide, to rest, in His pavilion of faith where panic and worry had no place. He took it all when He died on the cross for me…and for you.

Are you going through something in your life so overwhelming that you feel out of touch with your emotions about it? Something that has created such fear and confusion in your life that it has caused you to just shut down and feel numb? Dear one, you can find a place of safety and rest too. Jesus loves you every bit as much as He loves me. Matthew 7:7-8 says, "*Ask, and it will be given to you; seek, and you will find; knock, and it will be opened to you. For everyone who asks receives, and he who seeks finds, and to him who knocks it will be opened.*" The "you" in this verse means you! And the "everyone" means everyone! Jesus has promised this to you.

# Day 12

> The Lord always keeps his promises; he is gracious in all he does.
> Psalm 146:13b
> NLT

**From my journal**

We're standing on God's promises for Dwight.

Bleeding started out nose tube in evening.

*L*ooking back on this day I think God had me in a little cocoon, as it was really "the calm before the storm." I had even gone home to sleep the night after his surgery. He had a breathing tube inserted into his mouth and nose tube to drain fluid out of his stomach. He was receiving large amounts of fluids through IV to keep his blood pressure up and was heavily sedated; yet the doctors seemed pleased with his progress. His eyes were closed but he would nod when I spoke to him.

The next morning I sat in his room reading some email messages I had received from Aglow friends around the world who were praying for him. I serve as the Executive Director of International Fellowships at the Worldwide Aglow headquarters in Edmonds, Washington. It has been a joy to develop deep relationships over the years with Aglow women around the world.

One of the email messages was from my friend Sarah, the Aglow national leader in Portugal. She had been studying the scripture in Habakkuk, "*write it down and make it plain*" (Habakkuk 2:2). I realized the same scripture was part of that very word Dwight had received at the conference in our church a few months earlier—the prophetic word I had so boldly reminded God about, that first night in the hospital! I was so excited about this confirmation that God truly had a destiny for Dwight that was not yet fulfilled. I knew his life would not end before God's Word had come to pass. I just knew it. My God is not one to lie so I find rest in every word He speaks!

As I sat there reading, the anesthesiologist stopped by the room to see how his patient was doing. In our brief conversation I mentioned that Dwight was a very strong and determined man. The doctor's response was amazing.

He said, "Oh I know he is determined! I could tell even by how his internal organs looked and how his body responded during surgery."

He knew Dwight was determined! There were a million questions I wanted to ask about that, but was unable to take the doctor's time with them. We might think that if we talk bravely, or show courage or determination by our body language, that we will be a determined person. But even determination is a gift from God, imparted to the inside of us. It is a gift like other gifts that Jesus offers to us, as stated in 1 Corinthians 12; words of wisdom, words of knowledge, faith, gifts of healings, working of miracles, prophecy, discerning of spirits, different kinds of tongues, the interpretation of tongues. We can take those gifts and make them part of ourselves, or we can reject them, choosing to live in our own feebleness. Let us embrace every one of the gifts God offers to us.

*"But one and the same Spirit works all these things, distributing to each one individually as He wills"* (1 Cor. 12:11).

As the day went on, the doctor's concern for Dwight's condition grew. He had lost a lot of blood during surgery and his body was severely stressed even though the full surgery had not been accomplished. Now it was taking him longer than normal to make the initial recovery from surgery. His diaphragm had to be pushed up to remove the spleen, so his lung was partially deflated. The breathing machine was necessary to bring his lung back to capacity. I counted 14 IV medications, all running fluids into his body to keep him alive, plus the breathing machine.

By this time they knew this would not be a routine surgical recovery. They moved Dwight to another room on the surgical ICU floor, closer to the nurses' station.

The room was large with a long, padded window seat. I wanted to stay close so I had a pillow and blanket, intending to rest my body on that window seat through the night, even as I sought a place of rest for my spirit. I was having flashbacks to 1988 when I had spent many nights in a recliner by Dwight's hospital bed, wondering how long it would be before he could go home with me.

Very late that night, as the nurse and I were standing on either side of his bed, I was increasingly concerned because his condition seemed to be worsening. But I also knew it was that difficult post-surgery time. I was still hanging on to what the doctor had told me the day before, that Dwight would be able to go home in just a few days. However, what my eyes saw was making me feel afraid. "Oh God," I prayed, "Help me walk by faith and not by sight." (2 Corinthians 5:7)

The ICU nurse was efficiently and quietly checking all the IVs and tubes when suddenly the tube through his nose to his stomach turned red. Neither of us said anything. We knew what was happening. He was bleeding again. Soon the room was a beehive of activity as the medical team worked to do what they could to turn this situation around. They took Dwight off the blood thinning medication. He needed it to keep his blood from clotting, but it was also working against him, causing him to bleed in his stomach.

From that window seat I watched and prayed. My prayers weren't so eloquent. They were more like, "Oh God, please help us!" I was thankful that the nurses let me sit there in the room and I kept myself from asking too many questions so they could stay focused on doing all they could to keep my husband alive.

I remember feeling a "controlled panic," if there is such a thing. I reminded God of His promises. I was doing all I knew to do. "God—we're in trouble down here!" I called "the troops" for prayer. Over the next several hours I watched and prayed as the bleeding slowed and then stopped.

The surgeon checked on Dwight even through the night hours. He told me that the bleeding was "worrisome." It's not good when the doctor is worried! He told me something like, "We'll do our best to get him through this." I asked if he had a concern that he wouldn't be able to do that. He told me that my husband had been very sick, but had been getting better since the surgery. "Let's hope we can get him over this crisis tonight and that he'll keep on improving. Dwight is a very unusual case."

They transfused two units of blood and increased fluids to keep his blood pressure up. The heparin (low molecular blood thinner) was still off. The bleeding risk was obvious but that increased the threat of blood clots forming because of the Protein C disorder.

I felt as though I was hovering somewhere between nightmare and reality. I had no doubt that Jesus was with us and no question of God's love. I could find rest in that. But sometimes the unthinkable <u>does</u> happen, and I knew that all too well. I prayed that God would not send those angels to escort him to heaven that night.

So far Dwight had been transfused with 17 units of blood or plasma, plus the 600cc's of his own blood captured and re-circulated back into his body during surgery. By morning he had stabilized. The bleeding had stopped, he was fully sedated, but still on the ventilator (breathing machine.)

# *Day 13*

*L*iving in ICU is an interesting experience. Day and night are the same. The sounds of the breathing machine, mechanically delivering oxygen into Dwight's lungs and then exhaling in measured time, fill the room. The ceiling lights are always on so the nurses can do their work. Lights blink on the machines, IV alarms sound when a bag is empty, tubes gurgle when fluids are suctioned from his throat and mouth. I felt thankful for all those intricate machines that God had allowed people to invent. Each one was doing its part to keep Dwight alive. But I also needed a break from it all once in awhile. When I went down the hall to get a cup of coffee from the small family waiting room, the quiet was a welcome relief. And those "coffee runs" always included making several calls from my cell phone to keep family and friends informed of "the latest." I wanted everyone to be able to pray with understanding of what the current situation was.

The level of care was exceptional and the nurses were constant and consistent around the clock. I got to know each one who cared for Dwight, and enjoyed it when the same nurse would be with us for consecutive days. I trusted them, and really meant it when I told each one how much I appreciated everything he or she was doing for Dwight.

Pastor Dan and a couple of Dwight's friends from church came to see him. His friend Bob prayed that

Dwight would be surrounded by a "C" wall. (That is how Bob described the wall of Christ that surrounds us with His love and healing power.)

I went home that night to sleep and had a dream about Dwight. In my dream I was at the hospital, it seemed like I was in a corridor by the cafeteria, and Dwight suddenly came walking around the corner. He was a little unsteady on his feet but was fully dressed. He wore his work clothes—jeans, a navy blue shirt and suspenders. But I immediately noticed something unusual. He had sawdust on his right collar.

The next day Chaplain Robert came to see Dwight and I told him about this dream. He said, "Jesus was a carpenter. Dwight has been close enough to Jesus that he got sawdust on his collar."

# Day 15

> ...but with His own blood He (Christ) entered the Most Holy Place once for all, having obtained eternal redemption.
>
> Hebrews 9:12b

*From my journal*

It's difficult to wait for God's hand of healing to begin to move.

When a person is on a breathing machine, the machine is doing the work of breathing for him. In order to remove the machine the respiratory therapists first must do a "breathing trial" to make sure the patient is strong enough to breathe on his own. This is a torturous process that involves reducing the number of breaths the patient receives from the machine to see whether he will take breaths on his own between those mechanically given. The patient is awake so he can breathe but then the natural secretions in his mouth and throat make him gag and feel he is choking. It is an agonizing process for both patient and caregiver. As Dwight went through this process for the second time in as many weeks, I sat by his bed holding my own breath waiting for him to breathe on his own. The nurses allowed me to use the suction tube in the sides of his mouth to relieve his discomfort. They go through this process a couple of times, several hours at a time, before removing the breathing tube because they want to be sure the patient is strong enough and will not need the tube inserted again right away.

Dwight's body was being infused with massive amounts of fluid in order to keep his blood pressure from falling too low. In 15 days he had gained about 60 pounds, and had received 19 units of blood transfusions. The nurse told me Dwight's body was filled with 30 liters, about 60 pounds, of excess fluid. His progress was "inch by inch."

# Day 16

> Sanctify them by Your truth. Your word is truth.
>
> John 17:17

**From my journal**

Tonight the family gathered for all-night prayer vigil (+3 men from church) We stood firm on the Word of God. Prayed, read scripture, worshipped—did all we knew to do! (Dr. told me "it doesn't look good.")

*T*oday was our middle daughter's birthday. Dwight had come into the hospital on September 12, which was our oldest daughter's birthday, and today would also be a significant day.

The nurse told me that through the night Dwight had eliminated six liters of fluid—about one and one half gallons! His body was certainly being put through the paces. They wanted to get him off the breathing tube and did another breathing trial in the morning. He breathed strongly enough on his own but had a lot of trouble waking up. At 3PM the decision was made to remove the breathing tube. I had wanted this very badly as it was so difficult to see Dwight struggling so to breathe, but when the tube was removed and he couldn't seem to wake up, it was another great concern to me and also to the nurse caring for him. The tube had been removed and we were sure he would fully wake up soon. After that he would start improving quickly. Surely he would!

When you're in the hospital for a long time with a loved one, you yearn for anything normal. You wonder if life will ever be normal again so you are eager to grasp anything that feels like life as you once knew it. Our grandson, Christopher, 8 years old at the time, loves to be at our home and spends every weekend with us. It had been hard for him to know Grandpa was very sick and in the hospital, and to not stay overnight at our house as usual. This was a Saturday night so I decided to go home for the night (and take a shower and wash my hair!), pick up Christopher to stay overnight and bring him to church as usual, and then to the hospital to see his Grandpa. Dwight would be awake and we would have a nice visit—almost like normal.

Christopher was happy to be at our house, and even though Grandpa wasn't there we would get to see him tomorrow. He was already in bed when, about 9PM I called the hospital to check on Dwight. The nurse who answered the phone in ICU said that Dwight's nurse was in his room and couldn't come to the phone, and to please call back later.

I called again in a bit and was told the same thing. Then I knew something was not right. Finally the third time I called the doctor came on the line and told me

Dwight was bleeding again, probably from both his esophagus and his stomach. They had to re-insert the breathing tube. The doctor told me, "His options are not very good. It doesn't look good for him."

I phoned my daughter, Terry, and told her I was bringing Christopher home and she needed to quickly arrange care for him and come to the hospital with me. En route to the hospital we made urgent phone calls to all the family who lived in the area—Dwight's sister, two of his brothers, his mom, and our pastor. We didn't know what to tell them, except that Dwight was in great distress and we needed them to pray! Terry and I didn't speak much as we sped down I-5 toward the hospital. All we could do was utter short prayers shot heavenward like flaming arrows sent up to alert our heavenly allies that we needed help. Those prayers all seemed to begin with, "Oh God!"

Terry and I arrived at the hospital at about 10:30PM. When we reached Dwight's room there were five or six doctors and internists in the hallway outside of his room, all discussing his case. I later asked the nurse why all those doctors were there and he said whenever there is a traumatic case like this the word is spread and all the specialists on duty come to be ready if they are needed. I was grateful to every one of them.

One of the nurses spoke to me before I went into Dwight's room. She asked how I was holding up. She said she had lost her mother recently and understood the roller coaster of emotions. I looked at her, grateful for the human connection, but also unable—or maybe unwilling is a better word—to give myself into that place of sympathetic concern. I told her I was doing fine and was in a mode of intense focus. I think I said I felt "all business" at the moment. She said she understood… I'm sure they see every emotion and response imaginable in ICU!

What I meant was, I felt I couldn't spend time right then for my own tears and sympathy. I felt an intensity that demanded my full attention to the battle we were in. I believe this was the first moment that I realized the full scope of this war. It was an intensity demanding all my focus and strength, as when a woman is about to give birth. Nothing else matters except what she needs to do to bring forth that baby. That night nothing else mattered except what we needed to do to fight and win this fierce skirmish. There was no doubt that this was a spiritual battle!

To "fight" in prayer might seem like two concepts that do not go together. Many of us were raised in Sunday school learning sweet prayers asking Jesus to bless the little children and to gently lead us. But we must also know Jesus as He is described in Revelation 19:11-16. Jesus Christ riding out of heaven on a white horse making war on the enemy, Satan. Read those powerful verses and be filled with courage as you picture Jesus coming to fight for you!

We went into Dwight's room and, although they had cleaned it, we could clearly see the remnants of what had been a traumatic event. I was told that at about 9PM the nurse was right beside Dwight's bed, with the head of the bed inclined so he could breathe more easily, when suddenly he coughed a little and then violently vomited a huge amount of blood. Or at least it looked like a huge amount. The nurse, who had been a medic in Iraq during Desert Storm, said, "It looked like a war zone in here." I think the Lord blinded my eyes to this, but my brother-in-law told me later that he noticed bloody fingerprints on the monitors by Dwight's hospital bed.

By 11PM the family and several prayer warriors from church had gathered for what became an all-night prayer vigil. Our pastor had called our friend Bob, who rallied the troops and gathered several men to come to the hospital. All of these dear ones—family and friends —dropped everything and came in the middle of the night to fight with and for us. Amazing! We surrounded Dwight's bed and prayed, stormed heaven, declared and proclaimed. We did all we knew to do. Jesus of Revelation 19 was in our midst to battle with us.

One of the men from our church, Todd, encouraged me to lead in these prayers and proclamations. At first I felt timid to do this while surrounded by these mighty men of God. But then he reminded me that, as Dwight's wife we are joined together as one, so my prayers had the utmost authority in that setting. I pushed aside the feelings of timidity and stepped into the authority that I then, perhaps for the first time, really understood was mine.

When the nurses came in to care for Dwight we moved to the waiting room, just two doors down the hallway. We filled that small room and continued our vigil there until we could go back into his room again to pray. God had said Dwight had a destiny that He had not yet fulfilled! I knew I needed to continue to pray in my new found authority. That gave me new courage to remind God of His promise and to proclaim that it must come to pass.

I was anointed that night with power and determination from the Holy Spirit as I read out loud the Psalms God had given to me for Dwight. I read them over his body as proclamations of who God was to Dwight while the others laid hands on my husband, surrounding his bed and agreeing with my prayers.

From Psalm 71

*"In You O Lord, I put my trust…*

*Incline your ear to me and save me…*

*Be my strong refuge…*

*For you are my hope, O Lord God…*

*But I will hope continually, and will praise You yet more and more…*

*You, who have shown me great and severe troubles, shall revive me again…"*

And from Psalm 26

*"The Lord is my light and salvation; whom shall I fear?*

*The Lord is the strength of my life; of whom shall I be afraid?...*

*For in the time of trouble He shall hide me in His pavilion…He shall set me high upon a rock."*

I read and proclaimed again that prophetic word Dwight had received some months before that spoke clearly of his destiny.

By 7AM some of the group needed to leave, but we all felt we had done what we needed to do that night. Dwight was still alive. God was in control.

I deeply appreciated the attitudes of the nurses on duty that night and how they allowed us to spend time around Dwight's bed. We, of course, stepped aside whenever they needed to care for Dwight, but they allowed us the freedom to do what we needed to do also. I believe they recognized that we were not a bunch of "religious fanatics" performing strange practices. I believe they saw we were mature Christians with a purpose. Often in settings like hospitals people are afraid to demonstrate their faith, worried about what others might think. After that night not a single doctor or nurse commented negatively to me about what they witnessed from me or the many dear men and women who came to pray for Dwight. We had earned authority and we were walking in it.

# Day 17—Sunday, September 28

> *But God showed his great love for us by sending Christ to die for us while we were still sinners. And since we have been made right in God's sight by the blood of Christ, he will certainly save us from God's condemnation.*
> *Romans 5:8–9*
> *NLT*

**From my journal**

This was a scary day, and a day I was surrounded by love.

Scary news from doctors… Lots of loving friends came…Roller coaster of emotions as I faced having to make hard decisions for D's care…radical surgery? I'm full of faith, and full of fear too.

Just as I wrote earlier of determination being a gift from God, faith is also given at times for a special task. I believe I was given a "gift of faith" that Saturday night to pray and proclaim as I did. In his book, *Redeeming the Time,* Chuck Pierce says, "Faith itself is an event. It is the moment in which the soul of a man communes with the glory of God." (Page 179 Charisma House)

News had spread through our family and our church about what had taken place the night before, so the afternoon was filled with family and friends coming to the hospital. The waiting room, just down the hall from

Dwight's room, was filled with up to 15 friends and relatives at a time. They came to pray for Dwight, to love and support Terry and me. Our friends John and Michelle brought food for us, others gave me gifts of money to help with our food expenses at the hospital. It is usually easier for me to give than to receive, but all of those expressions of love ministered deeply to my soul.

I was grateful to our friend, John, for being my voice that afternoon and explaining over and over as new groups of friends arrived, what Dwight's current situation was and what the doctors were saying. He had worked as an EMT so he understood it all very well.

For our daughter Terry and me, the day was also filled with consultations with the doctors as they tried to determine their course of action in finding a long term fix for Dwight. That day "rest" was elusive as weariness and fear caught up with me and I cried all my tears that had been unshed the night before. Terry and I took turns consoling one another as we began to fully comprehend the situation.

Dwight was now fully sedated, with a Brighton balloon catheter inserted along with the ventilator. This balloon acts as a tourniquet to apply pressure from the inside of the stomach and esophagus to stop bleeding. I was told it is only used as a "last resort" because of the danger of it causing damage to the inside wall of those organs, which would then result in other serious problems. But we now were in a dire situation.

The Brighton balloon catheter requires traction to

hold it in place. I had been aware of this device since the first days we were in the hospital, when I saw a Seahawks football helmet on the shelf in his room! The nurse explained to me how the catheter worked. The end is tied to the face guard of the helmet to give the required traction and to hold it in place.

As it turned out the helmet did not work for Dwight because it didn't fit his head properly. So his nurse, Craig (the one who was the former medic in Desert Storm) improvised. When I went into Dwight's room I was shocked to see a long length of gauze tied to the end of the catheter at his mouth, then up and over an IV hook at the ceiling, weighted down with a full IV bag. It looked strange, but it worked.

And the catheter was doing its job. The bleeding seemed to have stopped.

About 1:00PM they deflated the balloon and performed an endoscopy to try to determine where the bleeding had come from. They were able to band and cauterize several places in his stomach and esophagus where the varicose veins had again ruptured.

Through the afternoon the reports to me were that they were considering a surgery the next day—one that is very risky and seldom performed; possibly the only hope for Dwight's condition. But first they had to be sure there was no more bleeding and no blood clots. In layman's terms, the surgery would involve severing the esophagus from the stomach, "stripping" the veins (similar to surgically "stripping" varicose veins in the leg) and then re-attaching the esophagus to the stomach. This surgery is rarely done, and had never been done on someone with Protein C deficiency.

"But God" I prayed, "how can I ever give permission to do such a surgery on my husband?" But God is sovereign. I could rest in that knowledge that He would lead both me and the doctors to make the right decisions.

That night, and for the next several nights, Terry and I slept in a family conference room that was located just a few steps from Dwight's ICU room. I was so grateful for a space that was dark and quiet. During the night both of us got up many times to go to Dwight's room. The nurses were so kind and always took time to talk with us. Terry sat for hours beside her dad's bed, holding his hand and talking to him. "He might be able to hear me and I want him to know I'm here," she said.

# Day 18

> *Wait on the Lord;*
> *be of good courage, and*
> *He shall strengthen*
> *your heart; Wait, I*
> *say, on the Lord.*
> *Psalm 27:14*

### From my journal

As we waited, another plan emerged—of aggressive banding. Has so far stopped the bleeding. The doctor said timing w/be important in this ongoing process.

*W*aiting, especially in ICU where time is often registered in moments, can be excruciating. After such an eventful 36 hours I wondered what might happen next. What decisions would I be asked to make for my husband? However, God's plan began to emerge. He was working on our behalf as I was resting, believing in Him.

That morning, Marcie, the nurse caring for Dwight, told Terry, "Your dad is a strong man… very determined." There was that word again. This was quite an amazing statement to make about a man under total sedation, on life support, and with tubes "everywhere!" The nurse said, "To live through two major bleeding episodes like he has, and be so strong, is amazing." And, Dwight's vital signs that day were normal!

By mid-afternoon I learned that Dwight's team of

doctors, all #1 in their fields, had decided not to do the radical surgery they had spoken of the day before. I thanked God I would not be asked to sign that consent form. The banding process seemed to be working and I learned it was actually a thoracic surgeon who would be doing "aggressive banding", a process of applying tiny rubber band-like "tourniquets" to veins that most other doctors would not dare to treat so boldly. I was told the endoscopies would need to be carefully scheduled because banding too frequently could also kill the tissue in the esophagus. The doctors felt they "didn't have anything to lose" (another disturbing thought) and were trying to keep from having to do the other extremely radical and risky surgery.

A plan had indeed emerged. I could feel God's hand resting upon us all!

# Day 19

> For in the time of trouble He shall hide me in His pavilion; In the secret place of His tabernacle He shall hide me; He shall set me high upon a rock.
> Psalm 27:5

### From my journal

The storm rages. Ps 27:5 He shall hide me & set me high upon a rock.

*W*hen I was a young girl growing up in Minnesota, there was a tornado warning one evening in the town where we lived. I can remember an eerie green sky and swirling clouds, even though the winds at our house were calm. I had quoted Psalm 27:5 in my journal on this day, and that scripture evokes the memory of that storm. You feel helpless in the face of something so fierce and huge, but in God we find our hiding place.

The doctors removed the balloon but told me they would keep Dwight on the ventilator for some time to allow him to just rest and heal. He still needed to lose a lot of fluid before he could breathe on his own. I was assured that he was moving forward, and even baby steps were progress. Thankfully, I didn't know at that time we were only one-third of the way through this journey.

# Day 22

> For He knows our frame; He remembers that we are dust.
> Psalm 103:14

**From my journal**

Yes Lord—You alone are our strength.

*W*e've all heard the phrase "Things tend to get worse before they get better." I don't think there is any scriptural basis for that saying, but it is human nature to hope for better days when things don't look very good. At this point Dwight's condition surely didn't look good but the doctors assured me he was doing well and it would get better. I hung on to their words and to God's promises, because what my eyes saw was very different.

It is at times like these—when what we see and hear do not match what we know God has spoken to us—that we must see and hear through the Holy Spirit. I knew it was wisdom to follow the doctor's skilled instructions and to allow all the medicines and procedures, but I also knew that what God had spoken was every bit as real. I thanked God for the skill of the doctors and nurses, for the medicines God had created for our use, and even for the machines and procedures used to carry those medicines into Dwight's body. But they were not the source of healing. God, in all His power and glory, was our source every moment of every day.

I sat on that window seat in Dwight's room, resting, believing in God's greatness.

It had been six days since Dwight had gone through that latest bleeding episode. The doctors had again greatly increased his IV fluid intake. It was necessary to fill his body with fluid in order to keep his blood pressure up but also to try and control the bleeding risk in his abdomen and esophagus. I didn't understand all of that, but what I did know was that Dwight's body now became so full of fluid I wondered how his skin could stretch enough to contain it.

He was partially sedated and on the ventilator. His legs were as hard and round as tree trunks and fluid "leaked" from his hands and arms at sites where IV needles had previously pierced his skin. The nurses kept towels under his arms that became soaked with the fluid his body could not contain. It had been nearly a month since he had eaten any food, but now he weighed 80 pounds more than when he was first admitted to the hospital. Eighty pounds of extra fluid in his body. It seemed impossible.

Pastor Dan came and Dwight opened his eyes at the sound of his voice. Pastor Dan and Pastor Doug were so good to stay in close touch with me and to come to the hospital often. Their love and support were life-giving to both of us. They and so many others were battling, so I could find rest.

# Day 23

> *And being found in appearance as a man, He humbled Himself and became obedient to the point of death, even the death of the cross.*
>
> *Philippians 2:8*

**From my journal**

Christ died in shame that we might be respected. Dwight's nurse—Paul—cared for him with great respect.

*I* have great respect for the nurses that care for patients in ICU. The doctors write the orders but it is the nurses who carry out the plan, and Dwight's "plan" was changing daily. The nurses, both male and female, all treated Dwight with great respect. I had brought a photo to display on the shelf in his room that showed the vigorous and healthy man that Dwight really is. The photo was taken out on Puget Sound on our little fishing boat and shows Dwight and our grandson Christopher, both in their matching leather cowboy hats, smiling at the camera with all the confidence and happiness of a man and his grandson out fishing. I wanted people to know who Dwight really was, not just as the man lying helpless in that bed. I wanted them to see a man who loved life and loved his family.

# Day 24

| *Submit yourselves, then, to God. Resist the devil, and he will flee from you.*<br>*James 4:7 NIV* | *From my journal*<br><br>God—take my thoughts captive!<br><br>Endoscopy but no banding needed. Full of fear. Full of faith. |

*T*he doctors were cautiously optimistic about everything. Watching for infections, bleeding…I waited and prayed. The promises of Psalm 71 and Psalm 27 were my daily companions. Many times a day I would turn to those Psalms and read them again. Sometimes out loud, sometimes only the lines I had underlined. Nearly always feeling great emotion as though I was facing down a great storm commanding it to go and leave us in peace. All of this was done quietly, using God's rest to battle in the heavenlies from my hospital room window seat.

While Dwight lay motionless and dependent on the ventilator, his friend Scott Rice came to spend the day by his side. Scott felt as I did, that it was important for someone to be close, especially while Dwight was unconscious. I had two meetings at the Aglow office that had been scheduled for a couple months, one with Esther, the Aglow leader from Costa Rica, and the other with Jane Hansen Hoyt, President and CEO of Aglow International, and the leadership team.

Scott arrived in the morning and stayed until I got back to the room at 7:30PM. Scott had been Dwight's advocate throughout the day. On this and many other days, he came to pray and sit with Dwight and me, with the heart of a caring friend, demonstrating Jesus' love for us.

# Day 26

> *I would have lost heart, unless I had believed that I would see the goodness of the Lord in the land of the living.*
>
> *Psalm 27:13*

**From my journal**

I am hanging on to that scripture. Lord let us again see the land of the living.

*T*his passage from Psalm 27 encouraged me not to lose heart. I believed that Dwight would live to proclaim the goodness of the Lord to our family and friends.

In my journal I wrote that he had lost 10 pounds of fluid since the day before. He was now off sedation completely but had not awakened.

# Day 27

> For You are my hope, O Lord God...
> Psalm 71:5
>
> **From my journal**
>
> It's Christopher's birthday.
>
> Sedation is off but Dwight can't wake up. Frustration & tears.

October 8, 2008—Today was our grandson Christopher's 9th birthday, and I had great expectation that Dwight would wake up today. I missed my husband! By the evening he was able to keep his eyes open and was trying to come out of the thick fog that held his brain captive. As I held his hand I asked him to squeeze my fingers. No movement at all. I gently asked him again to squeeze my hand. He couldn't do it and tears began to roll down his cheeks as he looked at me with no other emotion on his face. So we just sat there crying together. I had no way of knowing what he was thinking, but I was wondering what our lives would be like in the future. Or if there would be a future. Would he ever be "himself" again? Would he be able to talk, laugh, and communicate? Would he ever work again, or do any of the things he loves to do?

# Day 29

*This High Priest of ours (Christ) understands our weaknesses, for he faced all of the same testings we do, yet he did not sin. So let us come boldly to the throne of our gracious God. There we will receive his mercy, and we will find grace to help us when we need it most.*
   *Hebrews 6:15-16*
   *NLT*

## From my journal

Respirator removed in AM.
18 days since surgery

Dwight woke up today. Still under effects of sedation but came alive when we talked about ministry. Precious spirit in this man.

*Y*esterday and through the night Dwight seemed to be waking up more, so at 8:45 this morning the respiratory doctors removed the ventilator for the third time. They had done breathing trials and Dwight seemed to have the strength needed to breathe on his own. After the tube was removed from his windpipe his throat was incredibly sore and he wasn't totally coherent, but in the evening when our friends, John and Michelle, came we talked about praying for people and Dwight "came alive" with excitement. He loves to pray for people and see God move in their lives. I felt we were finally seeing progress.

Things were finally looking hopeful. Little did I know what the next 24 hours would bring.

# Day 30 — October 11

The Lord has made bare His holy arm in the eyes of all the nations; And all the ends of the earth shall see the salvation of our God.

Isaiah 52:10

From my journal

Intubated—4th time—midnight

Dr said, "It doesn't look good for him."

Not strong enough to breathe on his own..

Dwight lies in his hospital bed, naked & unashamed.

He has no other option but to trust. Twice over, the blood flowing through his body was given to him—but now he's made it his own. Jesus' blood made it ALL possible. LIFE

Statistics show it takes 21 days to develop a habit in your life. It had been 30 days since Dwight had been admitted into the ICU ward of the hospital and it seemed this had become my new way of life. I had been home about three times in all those days. Each time I went home to sleep I was urgently called back to the hospital.

It seemed every day held new dramas and I had a clear understanding in my spirit that we were in a spiritual battle as well as a physical one. It wasn't only that Dwight's condition remained so serious. There were times when I, as well as others who were standing with us in prayer, sensed a spiritual darkness in the room. Like a tug-of-war game being played between opposing forces. But this was no game, and we were fighting for life.

Many prayer warriors in our church and at the Aglow office also clearly felt the spiritual battle. I did not know it at the time, but even in his sedated condition, Dwight was also fighting a spiritual battle. It would be many days yet before the story of the dream/vision that he was experiencing could be told.

My days—my new way of life—consisted of rising from my rollaway bed in the corner behind Dwight's hospital bed at about 5:30 AM and quickly dressing to be ready to talk to the doctors when they came in about 6-6:30AM. (Do these men <u>ever</u> sleep?) Then I would get coffee in the ICU family waiting room, where I would usually see other family members who had also been there all night with their loved one. We would ask each other, "How's it going?" then speak whatever words of encouragement we could for each other. The Aglow office had sent me a huge fruit basket and others brought food also, so I didn't always need to leave Dwight's room to buy food in the hospital cafeteria. My days were spent sitting at that window seat answering a few emails on a lap top computer, between talking to the nurses and helping to suction Dwight's mouth when he choked on the respirator. My whole world was in that little ICU room. My whole purpose was using God's gift of rest to battle for my husband's life.

I am so grateful to the women I work with at Aglow International headquarters for giving me the freedom to do what I needed to do by staying at the hospital all those days!

I am also grateful to the hospital staff at Swedish ICU for allowing a family member to stay with their critically ill loved one!

What had begun as a day of hopeful progress ended far differently. Throughout the day the doctors were encouraged and positive about Dwight's progress. Physical therapists even worked with him a little. Although the sedation was still affecting him and he acted frustrated, I felt comfortable enough to go home that evening to shower and sleep in my own bed. On the way home I had a flat tire on the freeway! That had never happened to me before. My first thought was to call Dwight. He would know exactly what I should do. But I had to handle this myself. If I had been home in my driveway I would have figured out how to change it myself, but here on the freeway with cars speeding by, it seemed too dangerous. So I took advantage of our seldom-used roadside assistance. I was so grateful when I finally arrived home driving on my spare tire!

Before going to sleep I phoned the hospital and learned Dwight's breathing had become labored. I dressed quickly and, driving our other car, returned to the hospital, arriving about 11:00PM (an hour's drive at that time of night.) When I reached his room it was filled with people. The respiratory doctors had brought in the ventilator that seemed to fill the room, and were preparing to re-intubate Dwight. His nurse was there of course, as well as other nurses on duty that night that had cared for him at other times. They had gathered when they heard the news that he was being re-intubated for the fourth time, and they all were concerned. He had been off the ventilator for only 27 hours. Dwight was known throughout the floor as the man with great determination and strength, and they all felt so bad to see him go through this again.

When I reached the room the head of Dwight's bed was inclined to help him breathe. His face was red from struggling for air, his whole body shaking as he fought for each breath. The numbers on his monitor were too high for me to comprehend. His nurse told me to just not look at them.

Even as all the hospital personnel stood by, I put my face to Dwight's ear and, through my tears, proclaimed what I knew we both believed. "Determination, hang on, never give up! God is in control! He is our safe refuge! I love you!"

I wept as the ventilator tube was inserted. This time

they didn't even make me leave the room but I couldn't bear to watch. It brought life-giving oxygen, but also took my husband away to a place where I could not reach him. How long would it be this time?

# Day 31

> There is no greater love than to lay down one's life for one's friends.
>
> John 15:13 NLT

**From my journal**

Our friends are loving and sensitive!

Today Dave & Sandy are mowing and cleaning at our house, Scott & Kay are bringing me food, and lots of friends are praying!

The next morning the doctor explained it was not actually a huge set-back. However it sure felt huge to me! He explained Dwight still had too much fluid in his body and his lungs were like sponges, so he couldn't breathe. It would just take more time.

Time. More time. Now when I think back to those days, even I wonder how I spent my time day after day. Of course I wished I could spend my days anywhere else except that hospital. Every couple of days I would take a walk outside, and often would browse through the gift shop off the main lobby of the hospital on my way back upstairs. One day I realized the clerks in the gift shop were talking about me. "She's still here," I heard one of them say in hushed tones. "Yup," I thought. "I'm still here." And every day I wondered how much longer it would be before WE could go home. That was just it—I knew in my spirit that we had to go home together.

I'm not a naïve person, and I know that people do lose their loved ones to death—every day. Incredibly on this day, a Sunday afternoon while our friends Scott and Kay were with me in the hospital room, Kay received a phone call. Her mother had suddenly died in Redding, California. She had spoken with her just a few hours before as they arrived at church that morning. We both wept as we held on to each other in disbelief, praying for God's merciful presence to surround us.

I am aware, even as I tell my story, there will be someone who will read this and think, "I've been through tough times, too. I know exactly what that experience is like. My situation was even worse than hers. I believed as strongly as she did and I battled for healing too. But my loved one did die! Why?"

Dear one, I don't know why. When my daughter died I asked that question a million times. "God, if you'll just tell me why, I'll understand, and then I'll find peace." But He never answered that question. Instead He spoke something to my heart one day when I had—again— been crying out to God and asking Him "How long will I have to feel this pain? Just tell me why!!" Suddenly, He spoke to my heart "As long as it takes. I am in control, and I WILL walk with you."

I was stunned. That didn't seem very loving. "As long

as it takes? What does that mean?" Well, He didn't answer that question either. But I've come to know that can mean a very long time.

Walking through any kind of long term trial or painful situation isn't easy. It's hard, gut wrenching, a battle every step of the way. But I've learned something through the times of trial I've walked through. I've learned that God does stay close—"for as long as it takes" for me to truly come to that place of rest with Him. He laughs with me. He cries with me. He lives my pain with me because He has felt it too.

But through it all He asks, "Do you love Me? Do you love Me even now? Will you trust My love, even through this?"

And that propels me back to Psalm 27:8 *"When you said "Seek My face," My heart said to You, "Your face Lord, I will seek."* Yes Lord, I do love you! I run to hide in the high tower you have prepared for me. I find my rest in You—the only kind of rest that is truly real.

Once, several years ago as I sat in the back yard swing that Dwight had built for me—my favorite place in the world—I asked God, "What have I really learned from You through all of the things I've gone through?" He prophetically spoke these words to my heart.

"I am with you always—ready for you to lift unto Me the devastation of your soul, the weight of your grief, the sorrow you carry in your heart.

Let Me carry it for you.

Empty yourself of these things that weigh you down.

Give them to Me and fill yourself instead with My love. In My love you will find <u>rest</u> and peace."

Dear One, God did not cause all the things that have happened in your life. But He was there through every one of them.

# Day 32

> The godly may trip seven times, but they will get up again.
> Proverbs 24:16 NLT

The devotional today spoke about rising again and again, even if we fall; about picking ourselves up again and again, always living in expectation of seeing the miracles of God. This captured my attention because I know that is exactly how Dwight believes and lives his life.

I knew we were experiencing the miraculous hand of God with us in the midst of our circumstance. Here are some of the ways I knew this to be true:

Today Dwight had another endoscopy and the doctor applied seven more bands to dangerously bulging varices.

To date he has received 30 units of blood or plasma.

Cousin Shirley traveled from California to be with us for a couple days. Our pastors came. I received gifts of food and money that greatly helped during "my" long hospital stay!

The 80 pounds of extra fluid had finally been eliminated and his weight was now only one pound more than when he entered the hospital a month ago.

Two days ago the doctor told me, "It doesn't look good." But my husband is still here with us.

I count all these things as ways God kept His hand upon us!

# Day 34

> *And he said to them, "This is my blood, which confirms the covenant between God and his people. It is poured out as a sacrifice for many."*
> *Mark 14:24*

*From my journal*

All the blood that's been given to Dwight was made possible by the shed blood of Jesus.

*I* learned a new term today. The past few days Dwight had been extremely agitated and, although he had no strength to even lift up his head or his arms, his legs were constantly moving and he writhed around in the bed as if in pain. The doctor knew how concerned I was so he came and talked with me. This agitation was actually a condition called "Flash Pulmonary Edema." Dwight's body was trying to come off so many different IV medications, trying to breathe, trying to heal from the ventilator, and it all led to his body creating high blood pressure to push fluid out of his blood vessels and into his lungs. It is so amazing how our bodies react in times of stress!

Today I asked the doctor what was keeping Dwight so sick? He responded that Dwight isn't really sick, he needed to get rid of the massive fluid build-up they had pumped into his body to support his blood pressure and the massive blood loss. He told me Dwight had lost another 20 pounds in the past few days so that was good. They need to remove fluid slowly. "It just takes time," he said.

It seemed I was hearing that a lot.

# Day 35

> And He said to me, "My strength is sufficient for you, for My strength is made perfect in weakness."
> 2 Corinthians 12:9a

*From my journal*

Dwight lies in his hospital bed, his muscles soft and weak. I sit in this room, which has become my whole world. But when D awakes for brief times I feel the strength of his spirit. And I feel incredibly strong in God. How we love you , Lord.

Got off ventilator this evening after 5 days this time.

*N*ow, as all those pounds of excess fluid came off his body, Dwight began to look like "skin and bones." They say a person loses two percent of their muscle mass for each day they lie in bed. So he had already lost about half of his muscle mass and the skin hung off his legs and arms. We had to lift his arms to adjust the pillows under them. He did not have sufficient strength to be able to help us.

But our spirits and our bodies react far differently

from one another. There is no physical weakness in our spirits. As I've said before, this was both a physical illness and a spiritual battle. In his spirit Dwight was strong, and in time an incredible story would be told of a battle with the "Princes of Persia" that he experienced while he lay motionless in that hospital bed. When you read in Daniel 11 and 12 you know this refers to the anti-Christ spirit!

Satan, the ultimate anti-Christ spirit, is a liar and a thief. He will do anything he can to discourage and destroy the children of God. Dwight is part of the ministry team at our church and a student of the Wagner Leadership Institute, which is associated with our church, Sonrise Chapel in Everett, Washington. The enemy of our souls was trying to silence Dwight's voice and to discourage all the others who were standing with us. Much was at stake and that is why the battle was so fierce.

# Day 36

---

*Dear brothers and sisters, when troubles come your way, consider it an opportunity for great joy. For you know that when your faith is tested, your endurance has a chance to grow. So let it grow, for when your endurance is fully developed, you will be perfect and complete, needing nothing.*
*James 1:2-4*

*From my journal*

ICU Psychosis

Breathing tube is out—a new struggle begins. This is a real struggle—truly part of the war —but it will result in victory. God 's grace & mercy will bring it to pass—naturally (& slowly! Give us the grace to endure the process Lord.)

---

ICU psychosis—another new term I learned about. Dwight was awake (at least he appeared to be awake) and he could breathe on his own. He was trying to communicate but whenever he spoke his words came out in a jumbled rush of sounds that were impossible to decipher.

A doctor explained this phenomenon of ICU psychosis to me. He explained that in intensive care units there is 24-hour activity because patients need that constant 24/7 care. There is little, or no, difference in the activity levels between night and day. I could well understand that because I had been living in that environment myself for over a month!

But while I could find relief in taking a short walk outside or wearing night shades and ear plugs and sleeping through some of the middle-of-the-night poking and prodding, Dwight as the patient could not. And even when he was sedated he was not in a state of rest. So part of ICU psychosis is actually being sleep deprived!

This went on for days. Sometimes the nurse or I would hear a word we could understand and we would try to respond appropriately. I was careful to try not to guess too fast because Dwight would roll his eyes and just look away. He knew what he was trying to say!

But once in the midst of a string of garbled sounds I heard him say the word "chair." So the physical therapy nurse agreed to sit him up on the edge of the bed for the first time. He was able to sit up for about 4 minutes, with three people holding him upright. He didn't have the strength to hold his head up, but I bent way down to look at his face, and saw a tiny smile come to his lips as he sat there. Even small victories are important!

That one tiny smile was remarkable because for days there was no emotion in his face, delayed reaction and extreme weakness. All this was part of the ICU phychosis. I was surprised one day to realize his sense of humor was intact. I asked if he could hear me and he shook his head, no! But all with no emotion in his eyes or his face. It made me laugh.

Another time, Chaplain Robert had stopped by for his afternoon visit. The head of Dwight's bed was raised a little and the Chaplain and I were each sitting in chairs on either side of the bed. There were lots of pillows in the bed, under his arms and legs to keep them cushioned against bed sores. We were chatting quietly, not knowing if Dwight was hearing or registering at all with our conversation. Suddenly we saw Dwight make an awful grimace as if in great pain! No sound came from his wide open mouth, but we could instantly see he was in anguish. We both jumped and then realized Chaplain Robert had been leaning on Dwight's leg with his elbow—and it hurt! Chaplain Robert felt awful about it but at the same time we had to laugh. Dwight couldn't speak, but he could certainly communicate!

I knew my husband was still "in there" but how could he get out and be himself again? O God—You are my strong tower. I run to find safety in You. You are my rest, O Lord.

Jervae Brooks

# Day 37

| | |
|---|---|
| I was led to read this scripture for the second time in 3 days:<br><br>*My grace is sufficient for you; for My strength is made perfect in weakness.*<br>*2 Corinthians 12:9* | *From my journal*<br><br>ICU Psychosis<br><br>Dwight remains utterly weak in his body. But by God's grace his inner man remains so strong! If D can be strong, I surely can too! |

# Day 38

> ...rejoice in our sufferings, because we know that suffering produces perseverance; perseverance, character; and character, hope.
> Romans 5:3-4
> NIV

**From my journal**

ICU Psychosis

Clots in both legs

I'm not going to give up, but the struggle is intense.

Today I need to be reminded that I must persevere through this ICU psychosis. D has no facial expression, little response, no communication. I must not get impatient with it. I must persevere. I am weary.

Another Sunday afternoon and many friends came. Terry brought her three youngest children to see their Grandpa. We prepared them for what they would see, and they all bravely stood by his bed and talked with their beloved Grandpa, believing he could hear them. Our friends were interceding constantly, and Michelle said she was "praying her guts out" for Dwight!

# Day 39

> *But we have this treasure in earthen vessels, that the excellence of the power may be of God, and not of us.*
> *2 Corinthians 4:7*

## From my journal

This AM I was thinking—how long will this journey be? I wish D's progress could be faster. Oh Lord—I only want a God-ordained change according to His time. Help me to persevere & rest in Your holy graces.

*I*t was getting so hard to wait, day after day, for some glimmer of progress. I almost said, "glimmer of hope," but thankfully I always did have hope. I don't understand how that could be, except that God was there with me, walking through each day with me. He did that because I had invited Him to be there. God was my strength, and in that, I had the strength I needed to wait. It was all part of resting in God.

*I love you, Lord; you are my strength.*

*The Lord is my rock, my fortress, and my savior; my God is my rock, in whom I find protection. He is my shield, the strength of my salvation, and my stronghold.*

*I will call on the Lord, who is worthy of praise, for he*

*saves me from my enemies* (Psalm 18: 1-3).

Do you know that you have control over where your emotions go, or where your emotions can take you? When circumstances threaten to push you, emotionally, "over the edge" you can choose to take control over them. You find the strength to do that when you look to God, who loves you with all of His strength.

In Psalm 91:14 *The Lord says, "I will rescue those who love me. I will protect those who trust in my name."*

Finally, little by little, in very small ways, I watched Dwight begin to respond. It was amazing to me and I rejoiced at every tiny victory. I witnessed his determination and did all I could to help him.

He reached out for my hands and worked hard for a few seconds to pull himself up.

He looked at his fingernails after I commented they were getting long and needed to be trimmed.

He scratched his chin, and he pulled his blankets up with both hands.

These were amazing victories. He was slowly beginning to fight his way back.

# Day 40

> "Come to Me, all you who labor and are heavy laden, and I will give you rest."
> Matthew 11:28

*From my journal*

Dwight is finally really resting —sleeping! Thank you Jesus for calming his anxiousness.

This evening Dwight was finally sleeping, and I was sitting in a rocking chair that I had pulled to the side of his bed. But what should have brought peace to me, knowing he was resting, was replaced by, of all things, impatience. As I sat that evening by his bed, reading, his loud and forced breathing really got on my nerves. I wanted to tell him "Just relax and quit breathing so hard," but he was finally asleep and I surely couldn't wake him up to tell him that!

Finally I left his room and went to the waiting room for a while to watch TV. Just to get away from that noise of heavy breathing. I felt guilty, but annoyed.

I wrote in my journal...

*"I'm shocked at my feeling of impatience. Then God showed Himself.*

*He's been breathing hard through his mouth all day. Has little response or recognition. I'm worried, wondering.*

*Then I realized I'm impatient. This horrifies me. My God—*

*what's wrong with me! Just days ago he was on the ventilator. That was so much worse. Just before that he nearly died— probably more times than I want to know. And now I can't handle him breathing loudly through his mouth!!*

*I went to waiting room for a time out. Read some in a little devotional I hadn't picked up in a while. I read that waiting is a hard part of the testing process. Okay—that's what's going on. I'm being tested.*

*Nurse Melanie came in to tell me how she sees Dwight tonight (feels he is doing well) and mentions Oprah's show that's on tonight. It was coming on soon so I watched it. Was about the author of book <u>My Stroke of Insight</u>. About a brain surgeon who had a stroke and recovered. She spoke about what it was like to be unable to communicate and how she perceived the people around her.*

*I'm focusing on Dwight—getting him well again and how it might change him.*

*But I'm being changed too. "God show me how and help me understand."*

Dwight was still very sick. This evening he had pain and he couldn't talk. I was standing by his bed just looking into his face and the nurse, Melanie, was on the other side of his bed doing something with his IV lines. The room was dimly lit and felt peaceful.

As we stood there the nurse and I watched as Dwight reached up and touched my face. Then he raised his hand and looked up, as if he was looking at something far past the ceiling. He just stayed like that, with his hand raised and looking up to the ceiling for a minute or so.

It seemed like a very long time. The nurse looked at me with a question in her eyes.

Finally I whispered into his ear, "You can't go. You have to stay here. You still have things to do here." Slowly he lowered his arm and closed his eyes.

# Day 41

> *"...even there your hand will guide me, and your strength will support me."*
> Psalm 139:10
>
> *From my journal*
>
> Today Dwight had enough strength to blow his nose a little. Yesterday he couldn't do that.

That loud and labored breathing was getting worse. I began to think there was something caught in Dwight's throat. It surely wasn't a chicken bone, as no food had passed his lips for over 40 days!

I just had to find out what was making his breathing so labored so I finally took a flash light and a tongue depressor from the nurse's stand in the room. I made Dwight open his mouth so I could look in his throat. By now the nurses trusted me not to do anything foolish, but I hoped no one would come in just then and shatter my reputation!

It took a few tries to see into his mouth but I thought I saw something in his throat. I pleaded with the nurse to look and see what was in there.

WARNING TO THE SQUEAMISH—you might want to skip over the next two paragraphs!

The nurse thought she saw something too, so she

went to get forceps—and also brought in another nurse to hold Dwight's head still. I was standing close by, the caring wife that I am and I was accustomed to helping care for Dwight in any way I could. Suddenly the nurse yelled at me, "Don't look!" "Okay!" I said, and turned my head and shut my eyes tight as I heard both of these strong, brave ICU nurses exclaim as if they had seen something horrible. "Don't worry," she said. "We got the squirrel out!" "It was as big as a teabag!" the other said.

Apparently it is common for secretions to collect and dry in the throat and nose after being on a ventilator for an extended period of time. This wasn't the first time these nurses had performed this "extraction" of what they had termed a "squirrel" but they both said they never get used to it. No wonder! The next day, as hard breathing continued, I extracted the "squirrel's tail" from Dwight's nose!

Okay—too much information!!! But a little comic relief is okay too.

# Day 42

So he will do to me whatever he has planned. He controls my destiny.
Job 23:13 NLT

**From my journal**

No banding needed. Praise the Lord!

This AM I told D I'd dreamt he was healthy & talking. Immediately he began to cry. I haven't wanted to think this way but I did think of Job. Last night Pastor Dan said the devil will have hell to pay for all this. But I also know that God looks lovingly at D & says "That house is Mine." Dwight is in God's Hands. Nothing happens that He does not know about.

"Two steps forward and one step back," still does result in moving forward!

Dwight needed to get stronger, and starting to eat food by mouth would help that. Finally the nutritionist came to do a swallow test to see if Dwight was strong enough to eat food. If his throat muscles weren't strong enough to swallow properly the food could be aspirated into his lungs, presenting a whole new set of problems to deal with.

I was excited that this day had finally come, until I heard him refuse the spoonful of applesauce she offered to him! He politely told her, "No thank you. Not today."

I said to the nutritionist, "Please ask him again!" But I was told he probably really wasn't hungry because his body had been receiving nutrition through the IV's. So "I" had to wait another couple days before he was offered another spoon of applesauce. That time he accepted it.

That was a step forward. A step backward was the onset of encephalopathy (severe confusion) caused by high ammonia levels in his blood. His liver was not handling the toxins in his blood due to decreased circulation through the liver.

But there were some lucid moments that would suddenly come, and always took me by surprise.

Once Dwight said to me; "If the doctor asks you how I am, tell him I'm fine." But when asked if he knew where he was he said, "Yes, at Applebee's by the mall."

Another time the nurse asked him, "Do you want to sit on the bed pan?" "Not particularly," he answered.

But this evening he asked me to write a thank you note to everyone who had been praying for him. He said, "So many prayers." In his spirit, he knew.

## A special message from Dwight—October 23, 2008

*Yesterday Dwight was trying to tell me to "write it down" but I couldn't understand. Finally last night I got what he was trying to tell me.*

*He wants me to write to you all and thank you for praying for him. He said "there have been so many prayers." So, thank you with all his heart.*

*Your prayers are sustaining us, encouraging us, and moving the hand of God.*

*With much love,*

*Dwight and Jervae*

Amidst all of the activities of this day the spiritual battle was ever-present. When I went back into Dwight's room after yet another endoscopy, he was just waking up from the light anesthesia they had given him for the procedure. As I neared his bed he said to me, with urgency in his voice, "The atmosphere in this room is not good for healing!" So I closed the curtain on the door to the hallway and prayed a cleansing prayer, "sweeping" the room of any spirit that was not from God and inviting His ministering angels to fill every corner of the room.

In Ephesians 2:2 the scripture speaks of "*the prince of the power of the air.*" That is speaking of Satan, who lives in the atmosphere. And in Job 12:22 says, "*He uncovers deep things out of darkness, and brings the shadow of death to light.*" In prayer I changed the atmosphere in the room, driving out the darkness (shadow of death) and inviting in the light (Jesus.)

It had been an eventful day!

# Day 43—October 24

> As for me (us), I will call upon God; and the Lord shall save me.
> Psalm 55:16

**From my journal**

Got real food for first time.

Today D is trying to figure everything out. It's a very long & difficult road—back to health, back to strength.

But I do believe it's also a road that is moving us toward Him.

D is frustrated. Wants to go home. Needs to work hard in PT—to invest in his own deliverance from the hospital!

Today I was told that Dwight is now out of the first critical stage of needing life support and into the second stage of rehabilitation. I felt happy to hear this of course—for them to be talking about rehab he must truly be getting better. But the man I saw lying in that bed surely was a long ways from being able to do the required three hours of physical therapy per day!

It was October 24, forty-three days since Dwight had entered the hospital. And for the majority of those days he was heavily sedated and could not move his muscles at all. Dwight's body had been severely bloated with fluid for so long, masking the muscle loss that was occurring each day. Now, with the fluid retention reversed, his arms and legs were literally skin on bone, with no muscle tone whatsoever. It seemed the muscles were not even there anymore! Today he was given the okay to eat soft food, but he could not hold a spoon in his hand; he could barely lift his own arm or adjust himself in the bed. My once strong and robust husband was very nearly helpless.

But I want to encourage anyone who may be facing physical therapy rehabilitation, or loved ones who have watched as once-strong bodies are reduced to skin and bone. In your natural mind you wonder how can they ever become strong again? How can their bodies ever regain their former shape and vigor? I can testify that this is possible!

As the physical therapy technicians came two times each day they slowly and carefully helped Dwight to move his body and to strain his muscles to begin working again. I was told that, "Muscles have memory," and when they are forced to begin moving again, they will also begin to grow and strengthen. This is exactly what happened in Dwight's body.

At first it took two technicians and me to hold him upright to sit on the side of the bed. Now they were working with him each day to try and stand to his feet. It took several days for his legs to find their strength, but finally, with a technician on each side of him and a lifting belt around his waist, Dwight stood to his feet. We all cheered and he looked at me with a tired smile. I gave him a hug as we stood face to face for the first time in so many days. He told me he wanted to go home tomorrow!

# Day 44

> *I discipline my body like an athlete, training it to do what it should. Otherwise, I fear that after preaching to others I myself might be disqualified.*
> 1 Corinthians 9:27
> NLT

**From my journal**

Dwight's struggle is now a season of boot camp—learning to eat, stand, use his hands—everything. God wants it from him.

I know God wants from me to rely on Him alone—not on myself.

God consume me.

The excitement of standing to his feet yesterday was so tiring, Dwight slept nearly all day today. When he was awake he was very clear-headed sometimes, and very confused other times. My struggle was to keep my eyes on God, to rely on Him alone. I struggled to remain in His rest. There was absolutely nothing I could do to hurry the progress of healing. It was all part of the crash course on "training for reigning" that God has us on!

The nurses in ICU were so supportive and I had built a close relationship with especially those who had cared for Dwight most often. This evening I talked with his nurse, Craig, who had been one of the first to care for Dwight. He stopped in to see how we were doing, and I expressed my thankfulness for being allowed to stay in Dwight's room all this time. He confirmed to me that it is so important for family to be here in times like this, to encourage their loved one not to give up. I realize this is impossible for some families, but I also "know that I know" my constant presence made a difference to Dwight hanging on to life.

# Day 45

For He has rescued us from the dominion of darkness and brought us into the kingdom of the Son He loves.

Colossians 1:13
NIV

From my journal

Just before I read this I had written a page of notes about how far D has come in healing. And we (I) had prayed for the day & a new cleansing of this room. God has rescued us from the dominion of darkness. We are in the light.

*I* believe God's complete plan saved Dwight's life. Number one was God—overseeing it all, followed by all the doctors, nurses, medications, technology, love and prayers. And that was followed by Dwight's faith and determination. It all worked together *"for the good of those who love God and are called according to His purpose for them"* (Romans 8:28 NLT).

As I looked around the room I was so thankful to realize how much of the medical equipment I used to see near the head of his bed was no longer needed. The room was becoming more and more empty each day. Once there had been three IV "trees," all full of bottles or bags hanging from them. There had been 14 different medications going into Dwight's body at one time, all doing something to help keep him alive. Also the ventilator, suction hose, monitor showing many numbers that I didn't fully understand but knew they were not good.

Now there was one IV tree with one medication, an antibiotic. Praise God!

Another funny thing happened today to add some levity to it all. Dwight had been asking me many times, why he was so often being checked for pregnancy! I finally figured out that he must be hearing us talk about "protein C deficiency" and think we're saying "pregnancy!" Poor guy—going through all this and thinking he's pregnant too!

# Day 46

I pray that from his glorious, unlimited resources he will empower you with inner strength through his Spirit. Then Christ will make his home in your hearts as you trust in him. Your roots will grow down into God's love and keep you strong.

Ephesians 3:16-17
NLT

**From my journal**

Today for the 1st time D started trying to use his hands to do things for himself. I do believe that is in alignment with God's purpose for his recovery.

It was amazing to watch Dwight's determination to work through the extreme weakness in his body. With the help of two strong physical therapy technicians, Dwight stood to his feet two times today, and worked very hard to accomplish that.

In his spirit he was focused and determined. But his body was struggling with the toxins that were building up in his blood because the decreased blood flow through his liver was not cleaning his blood properly. This caused encephalopathy when high ammonia levels affected his brain.

This morning he seemed fine when one of the doctors came into the room and stood by Dwight's bed. Dwight was answering his questions but then said, "Doctor, why is my pickup in this room?" Dwight thought he was sitting in his pickup and the doctor was standing outside talking to him through the window of the vehicle!

At that point I was pretty concerned, knowing the doctors were thinking he would soon be ready to be discharged to a rehab hospital. Would he ever be able to think clearly again? Would I ever have my husband back as I had always known him?

# Day 47

For my enemies speak against me; and those who lie in wait for my life take counsel together, saying "God has forsaken him; pursue and take him, for there is none to deliver him." O God, do not be far from me; O my God, make haste to help me!

*Psalm 71: 10-12*

## From my journal

Ammonia level high.

This afternoon D said he didn't feel well. He told me he feels "the moment has come." The moment between life & death. All his numbers are strong. I read Psalm 27 and Psalm 71 to him. He asked me to sit & hold his hand & not talk to anyone right now. "It's important to me." So that's exactly what I did. He told me, "I want it to be just you & me."

The battle was continuing to rage. Tonight both of us could feel it almost tangibly in the room. In 1 Peter 5:8-9 it says, "*Stay alert! Watch out for your great enemy, the devil. He prowls around like a roaring lion, looking for someone to devour. Stand firm against him, and be strong in your faith.*" NLT

Dwight asked me to sit close to him and we just sat almost clinging to each other and praying quietly for a long time. Later when we could talk about this, we both had felt the enemy tried to make us think he could take Dwight's life tonight. NO WAY! We took a firm stand, in faith.

# Day 48

*...but I see another law in my members, warring against the law of my mind...*

*Romans 7:23*

## From my journal

Bleeding ...Endoscopy...
Liver specialist

There is a huge battle going on between D's earthly body & his spiritual body. At times today it was tangible. And the Body of Christ—all our wonderful friends & family—are battling w/us. Christopher is praying for his Grandpa.

$\mathcal{S}$piritual warfare can be a series of skirmishes. Again and again unexpected setbacks threatened the relative "peace" we felt concerning the progress being made in healing.

We recently had a visiting pastor from Fiji preach at our church. The title of his message was "Faith not tested is faith not trusted" It was a powerful message that we don't walk by sight but by faith. He was preaching from 2 Chronicles 20, about Jehoshaphat going out to battle, and said that even when God tells us the battle is not ours but His, we still have to go out onto the battlefield. At the close of his sermon the pastor gave us these truths to ponder:

> The battle is found on the battlefield.
> The victory is won on the battlefield.
> Faith is acted upon and tested on the battlefield.
> And the spoils are won on the battlefield.

Looking back to that day in the hospital, I recognize that, by faith, we had gone to the battlefield and, by God's grace, He won the battle for us. I am still pondering that in my heart, amazed at the power and goodness of God.

Today's blood tests showed high ammonia levels, explaining the confusion, but also very low blood levels. Seven units of blood were quickly ordered, 4 platelets and 3 red. They brought a respirator to the hallway just outside Dwight's hospital room and had a Brighton balloon catheter ready "just in case." Even the nurses, who had seen countless critical events, expressed concern for what was happening.

Dwight spoke a little. He prayed "God help me." And he said he felt he had nothing left. I made some phone calls to "alert the troops." Bob went to church and rallied everyone in all the Wednesday night classes to pray for Dwight. Scott Smith, another of the pastors at church, called and prayed with me over the phone. Scott and Kay Rice dropped everything and came to the hospital to pray. God had told Kay even before I called that they needed to rush to the hospital. They brought a CD player and worship tapes to play in the hospital room. We all felt the "full on" attack and our response in God was swift.

Later, sitting at my window seat I typed this email:

**From:** Jervae Brooks

**Sent:** Wednesday, October 29, 2008

**Subject:** I just have to tell somebody

*Things were pretty heavy around here today, with seven (not three as I first thought) units of blood being transfused into Dwight while waiting for the endoscopy. He was bleeding somewhere and two of the units given to him were plasma which helps to stop bleeding. His condition is well known around here and they aren't letting anything slide.*

*But I just was blown away by something and needed to tell somebody. So I thought of my dearest sisters at Aglow!*

*Dwight has had some pretty wild dreams while under sedation. And as he's told me about them I've been half amused and half alarmed as he spoke as though they really happened. One of them, that he's talked about a number of times, is of flying an airplane. (He said "put me in any kind of a plane and I can fly it!" Wow—that's news to me!)*

*But a story he's told me several times already involves the Crown Prince of Persia and his two brothers. Dwight knew that all three of these men were evil, and also that all three of them were dead. But others around were pretending these men were alive, even posing them to take pictures. Dwight told me he volunteered to put these three dead men in an airplane and fly them off somewhere. He said his plan was to drop them into the ocean!*

*But just now I read this email that had come awhile ago.*
**From: Lurdes M.**
**Sent:** Monday, October 13, 2008 5:18 AM
**Subject:** AGLOW MOZAMBIQUE
*Dear Jervae and Martha Stanley*
*Glad to have this time of sharing our beatitudes*
*to help us in prayer move, concerning about our*
*Country Mozambique. A war against the de-*
*monic power that rules Mozambique. The king of*
*Persia which controls our country Mozambique is*
*spiritual.*

*Does anyone but me get goose bumps? I don't think I'll*
*laugh about his dreams anymore. This tells me that Dwight*
*was fighting a battle in the spirit on some level while he was*
*asleep. No wonder he woke up so tired!*

*This is such a spiritual battle we're on. We both really*
*felt an attack last night and called some of Dwight's friends*
*to pray. Dwight was really feeling sick and even said "I feel*
*like the moment between life and death has come." That*
*scared me. The enemy of our souls wants to make us think he*
*can end Dwight's life. And if he can just beat Dwight down*
*enough he thinks he'll win. But we know Who wins!*

*Bye for now. Love, Jervae*

I received this response from Kathy, a co-worker at
the Aglow office.

*Oh my! I don't even know what to say. I can't believe*
*that Dwight has been on duty even in his 'sleep'. This really*
*shows how real the spiritual is. You can only hope that he*
*remembers some of this when he wakes. I guess this last battle*

*is what has caused the bleeding. Be sure to tell Dwight that even though he was flying their dead bodies…..he actually was in the battle that killed them. And…..that he did a good job and he shouldn't volunteer for the next flight…..tell him that Kathy will fly them.*

*And tell him to keep choosing life. We are all choosing life for him and for our nation. And for you, Jervae.*

*Love you, Kathy*

The next day we learned that a new vein had become enlarged in Dwight's esophagus and bled. It was successfully banded in the endoscopy last night. At this point the doctors were just waiting for the next bleeding episode, which wasn't the way they really wanted to manage Dwight's care. The surgical option called "devascularization surgery" was again explained to me. It was a very big surgery, rarely performed, and never before on someone with Protein C deficiency.

I prayed I would not be asked to make this decision for my husband. There were no more bleeding episodes throughout the night. Thank you, Jesus.

# Day 50

> But You, O Lord, are a shield for me, my glory and the One who lifts up my head.
> Psalm 3:3

**From my journal**

Today had to have another endoscopy & got blood. The storm continues.

D said (in a semi-sleep state) "What is the objective?"

I said—"To be in the will of God."

*A* line from today's entry in the T.D. Jakes devotional I was reading stayed with me all day. "If the storm comes and I know I am in the will of God then little else matters." We knew the storm was raging around us. We also knew God was with us. We were resting and believing.

As I was writing this, going through the notes I had kept each day because I felt that some day Dwight might want to know about everything that had happened to him, I honestly thought, "My God, is this ever going to end?" I knew I had lived it, but as I was re-telling the story it seemed almost bizarre that there was such a full-front onslaught day after day after day. If you've read this far—Thank you for hanging in there!

But little did I know that the enemy of our souls, who is Satan, was finally weighing his options and realizing he was NOT going to win this battle after all!

# Day 51—November 1

Michelle gave me this scripture

*"…Deep in your hearts you know that every promise of the Lord your God has come true. Not a single one has failed!"*

*Joshua 12:14b*

*NLT*

Dave Carson phoned and read Psalm 33 to me, which is all about the sovereignty of the Lord.

*From my journal*

Today was the day we called in the promises of God. Michelle I. got the scripture for Dwight. And today the fog lifted & he was back! This is the 1st day Dwight says he remembers since Sept 12.

Very early this morning Dwight woke up after a fitful night. He called to me from where I was sleeping in my roll-away bed in the corner. He was so confused about where he was, what was happening, why no one was around and no one was helping us. I sat by his bed and explained what I could about everything that had taken place during the past 50 days. I told him about all the wonderful doctors and nurses who were helping us, the surgeries, and the many blood transfusions. He listened, amazed, with tears running down his face. He asked questions and we talked a long time in those early morning hours.

Then we both dozed a little, me with my head resting on the side of his bed. When we woke up, he was back! The fog and confusion had lifted and he was Dwight again. I said, "I missed you!" He said, "I missed you too!"

During the night he had been in a spiritual battle with hopelessness trying to overtake him. It was like forces of evil were in the air. When we talked about it, it seemed to us like one last swipe of the enemy to try to make him give up. It didn't work, and the attack ended. It makes me remember what Kathy, one of my co-workers at Aglow had told me—the enemy's power is so limited and at some point he will know he has lost the battle. Well, he has lost and JESUS CHRIST IS THE VICTOR IN DWIGHT'S LIFE! Glory to God!

Dwight was still very weak and was working hard with physical therapists to be strong enough to leave the hospital and enter rehab. We were already approved by the insurance company for a rehab center in Everett, much closer to home. The doctor said, if all kept going as it was and he didn't have any more bleeding episodes, he would be ready to be discharged to rehab by the end of the week.

He was gaining strength daily. I watched him pick up a carton of milk from the table in front of him and bring it to his lips to drink it, and I thanked God. It was not many days ago he had not had the strength to do that. He couldn't stand up from the bed unaided, or walk without help yet, but even that was going much better each day.

Our hearts were so thankful, to God for His wonderful love and mercy, and to everyone for faithfully lifting us before the Father in prayer.

# Day 52

*I* was watching a miracle take place before my eyes. Dwight was helped into a wheelchair and we took a walk around the hospital floor. He had "lived" there for nearly two months but had never seen it. We stopped in the waiting room and had a cup of coffee. We had fun together doing these simple things. With the help of the physical therapists, he sat in a chair and ate his lunch by himself. He and I were able, unaided, to manage using the bedside commode—a huge accomplishment! We both were so grateful to God for it all.

# Day 53

Dwight was getting rid of lots of fluid. The nutritionist told me that the past month, from October 4 to November 12, he had lost 105 pounds! Being able to eat real food was accelerating the recovery. The doctors suspected Dwight had pneumonia, but then determined he did not. Thank you Lord!

# Day 54

> *And be sure of this: I am with you always, even to the end of the age.*
> *Matthew 28:20b*
> *NLT*
>
> **From my journal**
>
> We have not been alone. God has been with us every step of the way on this journey.

An associate of Dr. Johansson's told us he would talk with the doctor about a discharge date! We could hardly believe our ears when we heard those words.

# Day 55— Wednesday, Nov. 5, 2008

In the prophetic word that I received during that conference in our church which I have spoken of before, one line was "Arise O daughter of Zion and thresh. He is sharpening you in this hour to thresh for the harvest, for the Kingdom." It wasn't until months after Dwight's ordeal that I read the following scripture and realized how profoundly God had prepared me for the battle I would fight for my husband..

*You will be a new threshing instrument with many sharp teeth. You will tear your enemies apart, making chaff of mountains. You will toss them into the air, and the wind will blow them all away; a whirlwind will scatter them. Then you will rejoice in the Lord. You will glory in the Holy One of Israel.*

*Isaiah 41:15-16 NLT*

*From my journal*

Transferred from ICU to Rehab

We have both been forced (by God) to live through this process—all these 55 days in Swedish ICU!

*F*ifty-five days had passed since September 12 when Dwight was first admitted to ICU. Now it was November 5, just four days after he had really woken up and become fully conscious of his situation and his surroundings.

Today Dwight was transferred out of ICU at Swedish Medical Center in Seattle, to Providence Hospital rehab in Everett. I left my window seat, my place of restful warring in the spirit. It had served me well.

He was shocked at how weak he still was, but worked very hard at the rehab hospital, doing everything he was asked to do. He was determined to get strong enough to walk out of there.

On November 12 he returned to Swedish Hospital as an outpatient for an endoscopy and possible banding if necessary. But his esophagus was clear and no banding was needed. While there I saw the gastroenterologist who had attended Dwight that first day back in September. As we briefly recounted the events of the past two months he told me, "I believe in miracles." When we parted he told me I had made his whole day. Mine too!

On November 14 Dwight was able to go on an outing with the therapist to test his skills out in public. We scheduled it for a Friday morning so Dwight could meet the men from church at the restaurant where they have breakfast and Bible study after the Friday morning men's prayer time. Our pastor knew he was coming but the others were surprised. They stood and applauded when he walked in! It was a very moving moment for us all.

On November 23, 2008 I wrote a Thanksgiving letter.

Here are excerpts…

*Dearest Family and Friends,*

*Happy Thanksgiving greetings to each of you!*

*We have been in touch with some of you with an update of Dwight's progress, but I felt I needed to write to you all to be sure I haven't missed anyone! We are so very grateful to each of you for your love and all your prayers. We could not have made it through these past nearly three months without them!*

*Dwight came home from the rehab hospital last Saturday afternoon, November 15. They had expected he would need to be there two to three weeks to regain his strength enough to come home, but they released him after only one and one half weeks. As he had determined to do, he walked out using only a cane. I followed him and the nurse, pushing the wheelchair. He was still weak, but he had proved he was able to manage well enough around the house, dressing, bathing, and eating his meals.*

*Now, after being home for a week, he is getting stronger every day. He only uses the cane when walking outside, and he is diligent about doing all the physical therapy exercises. Last Sunday he was so happy to get to church for the first time, but only had strength to sit during the whole service. Today he stood during worship and even went forward to pray with a few people during the ministry time. Dwight is back!*

*It has been only about three weeks ago that he could barely lift his hand off the bed, and to watch him do all these things, even eat by himself, is a wonder to my eyes. I am so thankful to God for allowing Dwight to remain with us here on this earth. Thank you, THANK YOU, for all your love and your prayers.*

*Dwight wants me to tell you that he is deeply grateful for your prayers. He will continue now, in God's strength, to keep on ministering where he left off. He knows God has touched him in a special way.*

# Epilogue

When Dwight was released from the hospital his medication regimen included a liquid called Lactulose (also called Enulose.) The liver specialist told him he would be taking this for the rest of his life! Because of the decreased blood flow through his liver, toxins would build up resulting in raised ammonia levels in his blood. When ammonia forms in the blood and reaches the brain, a condition called encephalopathy (severe confusion) results. If left untreated it can lead to loss of memory, then coma and ultimately, death. Even when taking the prescribed dosage of Lactulose, the risk of this happening is fairly great and so Dwight was told he could not drive a car. This took away any hope of returning to his job as a truck driver for a local petroleum delivery company. As you can imagine, this was hard for both of us. When I was at work he felt trapped at home, and also fought the fear of becoming encephalopathic and not realizing it. After all, if you are severely confused, how do you know to tell anyone?

We learned how frightening this is one month later, in December. A medicine cup we had been using to measure the Lactulose liquid was a little smaller than it should have been, and so for a couple weeks Dwight was unknowingly taking slightly less of this medication than he needed. Looking back I recognize some signs that he was not doing well, but at the time I didn't realize it. We had invited some friends for dinner after Christmas with the promise that Dwight would make some of his "famous" barbequed ribs. He had made these many times, and they were always delicious. But this time he completely ruined the first batch, and we had to go out and buy more meat to make them again. He really had trouble making this dish, and the meat we served to our guests that night was not as special as we hoped it would be. But I did not recognize this as a sign of trouble brewing.

Early the next morning, December 30, I woke up to find Dwight in the bathroom, unable to remember how to walk back to the bed. I did manage to get him in bed, and called 911. The medics came and he seemed fine. When they asked him if he wanted to go to the hospital, he told them "No, thank you." They had to abide by his choice at the time, so they left.

We slept for another hour or so, but woke when Dwight fell out of bed and couldn't figure out how to get to his feet. I called 911 again and this time they, too, saw the confusion. We spent the day in the emergency room, and then he was admitted to the hospital. He only had to stay one night, until they got his ammonia level under control. But it left us both shaken and scared about what the future held for him.

Our friend, Scott Rice, was going to be in Redding, California, at their home there, and on January 8, 2009 bought a plane ticket for Dwight to fly down for a few days. They were visiting the Healing Rooms at Bethel Church, and later, while in the church bookstore, were surprised when a woman they had just met gave them tickets to the evening sessions of the Randy Clark healing school to be held at Bethel Church the next week. There had been no tickets available but God wanted them there! I was a little surprised when Dwight called me to talk about staying a week longer than planned, but I knew he was in good hands with Scott. I was happy for him to have this experience and this pleasant time away from hospitals and doctors.

Dwight and Scott had many wonderful and amazing times together that week, with God in the midst of every conversation and all that they did. When the evening sessions began it was exciting for both of them to be there to take part in the vibrant praise and worship, wonderful teachings, and extravagant faith-filled prayer times. Dwight decided he would go forward for prayer at every single opportunity, knowing and believing that when he hit the "tipping point" he would be healed.

Session after session he went forward for prayer. While in line waiting to enter the sanctuary before a session, people standing near would pray for him. Whenever there was prayer happening, Dwight put himself in the middle of it. Always expectant. Always believing.

The last session they attended was the evening of January 15. During that session the students of the School of Supernatural Ministry at Bethel were asked to come to the front and to speak out words of knowledge as the Lord gave them these words. The congregation was instructed to respond by going to the person who spoke a word of knowledge that applied to them, and receive prayer to take hold of that word for themselves.

Dwight heard one young man call out a word of knowledge that God was going to heal someone's liver. He felt it was for him and began moving through the crowd looking for the young man. But before he could find him, a group of three or four men spontaneously gathered around Dwight and began to pray for exactly what he needed. Suddenly a young man, 20 or 22 years old, walked up and pointed at Dwight. He said, "God is doing something in your liver right now!"

Dwight didn't feel any different, but he hung on to every word by faith.

On January 20, 2009, four days after returning home, Dwight had an appointment with Doctor Johannsen. I was traveling for Aglow that week so Scott brought Dwight to the appointment. I was praying for him from Europe and couldn't wait to talk with him. Dwight told me that when Dr. Johannsen walked into the examining room the doctor took one look at him and said "I want you to cut back to one-half dose of Lactulose." As a specialist the doctor could recognize signs of improvement. That was music to our ears!

On January 27 Dwight went for another endoscopy and received an "all clear." There were no protruding veins in his esophagus. On January 29 he began decreasing his dosage of Lactulose, under doctor's supervision, and after I was home to be able to watch him for any signs of encephalopathy. There were none.

On March 20, 2009 he took his last dose of Lactulose

and has had no sign of liver dysfunction since! All praise to our Heavenly Father, who holds us in His strong hand through every situation in our lives.

As I put the finishing touches on this story it is January, 2010, and Dwight is in Thailand on a mission trip! We had both been praying that he would have an opportunity to be part of a mission team from our church. When this trip was announced at our church we both felt it was right for him. Thankfully, his doctor agreed. The team visited refugee camps on the Myanmar-Thai border and orphanages in northern Thailand.

During that period of time when he was far away from his doctors he needed to seek the peace of God. If he were to need medical attention the doctors there would likely not know how to treat his condition. But God heard his prayer, filled him with peace, and he had no fear because God gave rest to his soul.

And so, we continue to live our lives, thankful for each new day. As Christians we know that walking with God is an eternal journey, ever changing, always new.

# Part III:

## Rest

I sub-titled this book "55 days of warfare and rest" because God has taught me about both during this journey of the past couple years. I have learned that resting isn't just sleeping late in the morning, or lounging in a hammock in the back yard! Rest is a powerful tool in our hands, as God uses it in many ways to guide and shape our life.

Rest is an attitude, a demeanor we can surround ourselves with. Rest is walking in faith. There will come times of tears, anguish, and even stress. But if we make a conscious decision to accept God's rest, that powerful tool can be ours.

In the story of our 55 days in the hospital, I did my best to describe that season of our daily spiritual warfare, intercessory prayer, and contending for the promises of God. But underlying it all was the power of rest, as God created it for us. I felt this during the many hours I sat next to Dwight's bed, or in that window seat in his hospital room. I call it a "powerful rest." Even when I was sitting quietly, even peacefully, I felt God's power in me and in the room surrounding us.

Recently my friend Lilla, who serves as the national leader of Aglow in Hungary, shared a beautiful teaching from the Song of Solomon. I asked her if I could share some of it here, and she gave me her permission.

Song of Solomon 5:2 says, *"I slept but my heart was awake."*

Lilla said that unusual phrase captured her thoughts and she asked God to help her understand what it meant.

She shared that sometimes she goes to bed earlier than her husband. She knows he is coming soon, and she goes to sleep, but she misses him lying in the bed beside her. She might be sleeping, but her heart is awake and longing for him to be with her.

When she talked about this I thought of all those many nights when I went to my roll-away bed in the corner of Dwight's hospital room. To close out the light I put night shades over my eyes, and to get some relief from the noises I put plugs in my ears. This allowed me to go to sleep, but I longed to lie with my husband beside me and so my heart was awake.

This is how the Holy Spirit feels about us. He longs to be close to us, and He longs for our hearts to be fully awake to Him. This "awake ness" is full of peace, of resting in God. It is a place of perfect safety. Fear and frustration have no place in the beautiful rest that God has for us.

So resting and being awake do go together. We can rest in God's peace and at the same time be awake in our spirits to hear His voice.

# What else is Rest?

Once I took some vacation days from work to just stay home and "rest." My plan was to spend a day sitting outside relaxing and reading, and then I planned to get busy and paint some walls in our house. I decided to spend part of the week resting, and part of it accomplishing some tasks around our home.

The first morning I woke up and before I got out of bed I asked God to lead me in this week of rest. But I said to Him, "What is rest, Lord?" Our lives are so full of doing good things, but in doing all these good things, we work and stay busy until we are exhausted. I asked God to help me learn about what rest really means.

So I went to Webster's Dictionary. The first definition of rest is: minimal function, freedom from activity, peace of mind and spirit, renewed vigor. I thought that sounded pretty good. That was for me!

The second definition said rest is: to sleep, lie down, cease from action or motion, to be free from anxiety or disturbance, to remain confident, trust. That definition sounded a little more spiritually relevant.

But the third definition was very unusual and really caught my attention. It said "a rest is a projection or attachment on the side of the breastplate of medieval armor for supporting the butt of a lance, or a sword." This was very interesting! I got excited and felt God wanted to show me something in this.

So I got my note pad, Bible, cup of coffee, and was

excited to study scripture and write down things I felt God would show me. I got myself all set to accomplish something with this word.

I was literally sitting with pen in hand when suddenly Jesus spoke clearly to my heart. He said "Finally I have you alone with Me." I burst into tears, and repented for being too busy for too long. So busy doing things for Him—good things—but not stopping just to be with Him.

At that time Dwight and I had been married for 38 years. We talk a lot but some of the most precious times are when we just sit together. Jesus wants that with us too.

Jesus really wanted to teach me about rest. I didn't paint any walls that week. I didn't do much of anything. I sat and looked at the trees and flowers in our yard, felt the sun and the breeze on my face, read, took my grandson to the beach…I spent a peaceful week with Jesus.

# Rest and the Full Armor of God

I want to share more about that third definition of rest from Webster's Dictionary. When I was in Spain a few years earlier for their Aglow conference, I was taken on a tour of the palace in Madrid. While at the palace I saw the king's armory. Here they have a large display of the armor that had been worn by both the soldiers and their horses in days gone by.

The soldiers also carried large, heavy swords to be used in battle. In order to carry them while they were riding on a galloping horse, they had a projection of metal sticking out from their armor on which they could hang the handle of their heavy sword. So, as I've already said, this projection from the body armor—or breastplate—is called a "rest" and is for supporting the butt of a lance or a sword.

I think that is so interesting. In the natural a sword is a tool of war. But, when being carried by a soldier wearing body armor, it needs support of something called a "rest." And in the spiritual realm, rest is also a powerful tool of war.

I began to search out scriptures, first about breastplates that support this "rest." I found that the word "breastplate" is used 28 times in the New King James Bible. One of these is in Isaiah 59 where we read "*For He put on righteousness as a breastplate.*" And in Ephesians 6 it says "*Stand therefore, having girded your waist with truth having put on the breastplate of righteousness.*" And I Thessalonians tells us, "*but let us who live in the light think clearly, putting on the breastplate of faith and love.*"

Just from these few scriptures we can see that this breastplate represents righteousness—vital to helping us walk in integrity. It also represents faith and love, and most importantly, strength to stand—even in the midst of battle.

In today's world it is all too common to be in the midst of some kind of battle or another. That battle might be taking place in your home, or in your work place. It might be taking place inside your mind, threatening to rob you of a victorious walk with God. Or it might be taking place in a hospital room in the intensive care ward!

During medieval times when this armor was worn, it protected the vital parts of the body during battle. Today we use bullet proof vests, armored tanks and bullet proof glass. The vivid picture of this body armor helps in our understanding of the importance of the full armor of God.

Ephesians chapter 6 gives us keys to the spiritual understanding of the importance of armor. In verses 13-17 we read: *"Use every piece of God's armor to resist the enemy in the time of evil, so that after the battle you will still be standing firm. Stand your ground, putting on the sturdy belt of truth and the body armor of God's righteousness. For shoes, put on the peace that comes from the Good News, so that you will be fully prepared. In every battle you will need faith as your shield to stop the fiery arrows aimed at you by Satan. Put on salvation as your helmet, and take the sword of the Spirit, which is the word of God."* NLT

That spiritual body armor, and especially the breastplate of righteousness, was vital to me in the season of spiritual warfare that we were in throughout Dwight's illness. This piece is so important to wear at all times because, in the natural, it protects our heart and our vital organs. And we need that same protection spiritually too. While we were in the hospital, Satan tried to attack my spiritual heart—my faith and resolve. Because our heart is the seat of our emotions and all that is closest to us— family, sense of self worth, even trust in God—Satan knew if he could destroy my spiritual body armor he would win a victory over Dwight and me and everyone else who was praying for us. But God's righteousness is the body armor that protects our heart for God, and that is powerful!

As I have said, Psalm 71 was a great place of refuge for me throughout Dwight's hospital stay. Verse 2 reads *"Deliver me in Your righteousness, and cause me to escape."* God provided a breastplate of righteousness for me to hide in, and here it even speaks of it being a source of deliverance. Isn't God amazing!

# Rest in Confidence

We are all in a spiritual battle with Satan trying to break down our trust and hope in God. He is trying to destroy our heart and make us feel like orphans. But we are NOT orphans! We are beloved sons and daughters, and we can trust in that. We can know that God approves of us because He loves us so much He sent His Son to die for us!

I have heard Graham Cooke speak about this. He says, "God is absolutely delighted with you. You can walk confidently before Him. God has no anger toward His children because He spent all His anger on Jesus." The first time I heard that I was amazed at the thought of God spending all His anger on His beloved Son Jesus. What love for us! What confidence that instills when we really "get it" that we are loved so much!

I have a friend who told me about a horse she owned. She loved to go riding, and the horse loved it too. But the area where she most often had to ride was filled with countless holes in the ground from ground hogs. She had to be careful to steer the horse away from those dangerous areas, and the horse also sensed the danger. If he stepped in one of those holes he would break his leg. So she could never let the horse run as it wanted to.

But one day she had an opportunity to take her horse to a race track. It was a well groomed track with deep loose dirt, perfect for running horses at top speeds. She was excited to finally let her horse really run!

She said they started around the track and her horse stepped carefully as he had learned to do. She coaxed him to go faster, so he went into trot. As he went along, feeling the soft, safe ground under his feet with his rider coaxing him to go faster, he suddenly seemed to understand it was a safe place. She said it was the most amazing feeling when he realized it was safe to run as fast as he wanted. And run he did! Horse and rider flew around the track with joyful abandon.

If we are scared and unsure, too afraid we will fall down, too afraid we'll get hurt, we will never walk in confidence. We will never be able to run as a horse in full gallop on a safe track! But when we are utterly confident of God's unending, limitless love for us we can fearlessly walk and run with God as our strength.

We <u>can</u> walk in wholeness. I believe this with my whole heart. We can live our lives in the protection of the righteousness of God. We need to consciously put on the breastplate every day. It is our right. It is our gift. It is our protection given to us by our Heavenly Father. And if we are in the midst of the battle, it is our very life.

# Rest is a Weapon

And, our armor includes another weapon—the sword. This we know represents the Word of God.

The sword is the only weapon of offense in the list of armor. I have described many days and nights when I used my sword, the Word of God in the Bible, to take the offensive against Satan.

Here is a powerful quote from Bill Johnson's book, *When Heaven Invades Earth.*

"The authority to cast out demons is found in rest. Rest is the climate that faith grows in. It comes out of the peace of God and it is the Prince of Peace who will crush Satan under our feet. What is restful for us is violence to the powers of hell. That is the violent nature of faith… This is not a soulish attempt at self-confidence or self-determination. Instead it is a moving of the heart into a place of surrender. A place of rest. A surrendered heart is a heart of faith. And faith must be present to please God." (Page 54 Destiny Image Publishers)

Rest is a powerful weapon! We can use rest and faith to cast out the demons assigned to destroy our family, and to surround ourselves with God's protection. I used rest to stand against the demons assigned to take my husband's life. Faith cannot be self-will, trying to manipulate God to do what we want Him to do. But when we honestly act in faith, we are pleasing to God. Faith doesn't create the will of God, it releases it. Faith in God is our way of joining God in what He wants to do. And it is released when we join God in what He is doing. When we activate, through faith, what has been given to us, then we will join in the will of God.

You can do this in your life too! Power comes with rest. If you want power and vitality in your life, it comes through rest and relationship with God.

# Rest—and Doubt???

Dwight was in ICU for 55 days. That is a long time. Day after day, when things were not going too well, or worse, of course I wondered what was going to happen. I never lost my faith and hope. But I also have to be honest and admit that I did have times of doubt. How does this affect our prayers and how is it related to rest?

Doubt is an interesting concept that shows up in some unexpected places in the Bible. Did you know that just before Jesus gave the disciples the Great Commission, even though they had seen his resurrected body with their own eyes, some of them still doubted? Matthew 28:17 reads: "*When they saw him, they worshiped him—but some of them doubted!*" (NLT). That sounds shocking to me. But the disciples were men like you and me, and in their minds they could not comprehend what they were seeing with their eyes.

God is not limited, even if we have doubts. He taught me this in 2004, right after I had breast cancer surgery. I had an opportunity to travel to Israel on the Aglow tour, and wanted very much to visit the Holy Land. Two months before the tour was to begin, I received the diagnosis of breast cancer. The day I met with the surgeon I told him I planned to travel to Israel just one month after the surgery date. He said, "We'll see."

Before the surgery my Aglow sisters prayed for me and one of the prayers was from Mark 11:23. Jesus is speaking and says, "*I assure you that you can say to this mountain, 'May God lift you up and throw you into the sea;' and your command will be obeyed. All that's required is that you really believe and do not doubt in your heart."*

The surgery went well. It was a small tumor, fully contained and the pathology report showed the tissue was clear around it. I felt confident all was well, and must admit I rather enjoyed the week at home after surgery with doctors orders to stay in bed and do nothing.

I thanked God for His healing to be completed in my body, and prayed believing I would get the doctor's approval to travel to Israel with the Aglow group. As I prayed about Israel I thought of that scripture in Mark. "*All that is required is that you really believe and do not doubt…*" I thought, "God I do really believe! I believe You will clear the way for me to go. But how do I not doubt?" It's like telling a child that if he doesn't stick his tongue in the spot where his tooth has fallen out, a gold tooth will grow there. The child doesn't know it isn't true, and he determines to have that gold tooth! But then suddenly, before he even realizes he's done it—his tongue is in that empty spot. It's done and he can't take it back!

We say, "God I will not doubt." But suddenly a doubt comes into our mind. It's quick and fleeting, but a doubt nevertheless. So is all hope now dashed, for that one doubt? Heavy questions for a week at home 'resting' in bed!

It was Easter week so I decided to read the Easter story in all four of the Gospels. That would be more uplifting than wondering about doubt! But as I read them

I was surprised to find that word "doubt" in all four of those accounts. This led me to do a word study of that word "doubt." And what I discovered freed my heart.

In Mark 11:23, the Greek word for doubt is pronounced "dee-a-kreeno." This word refers to "doubt in your heart." (And actually, the scripture says just that in the New Living Translation.) Some of the definitions are: to separate thoroughly, to withdraw from, oppose. It means: I don't believe it! In my heart I turn away from it.

Then I searched out the word doubt that was used in the other Gospels (Matthew, Luke and John) and found that it was a different word in the Greek. It is pronounced "distadzo." This word refers to "doubt in your mind." Some of the definitions are: to waver in opinion, to doubt in mind. It means: I don't understand this, but I still do believe it.

So the disciples did doubt, but their doubt was "distadzo." They believed, they just didn't understand. In Luke 24 Jesus appears to His disciples for the first time after the crucifixion. Verse 41 says, *Still they stood there doubting, filled with joy and wonder.*

In the hospital, my doubt was "distadzo" doubt. I believed God would heal my husband, but I did not understand how it would happen.

Beloved, we need to use the Word of God as a sword. Use it to cut through and clear the way. Clear away doubts, anger, worry, insignificance. Just as it cleared the fear of doubting out of my mind.

I did receive the doctor's approval to travel to Israel,

four weeks after surgery, and had a wonderful time! The Word of God was used as a sword to cut away the fear of doubting. This was so freeing to me at that time.

And likewise, when I had feelings of doubt creep into my thoughts while in the hospital with Dwight, I knew I did not need to fear.

# Rest—It's Greek to Me!

In my word study about "rest" I came across an interesting note in the glossary at the back of *The Power New Testament—Revealing Jewish Roots*. It says there are three Greek words that are translated as "rest."

Epanapauomai—means to lean upon, to trust in something.

The other two are used much more often, but there is a major difference between them.

Katapausis—is the permanent rest of the eternal kingdom. The "rest" spoken of in Hebrews 4 is this word. But this is not only the eternal rest we'll find in heaven. It is also the constant place of rest we should dwell in spiritually.

And the third Greek word for "rest" is—Anapasis—a temporary rest, like a coffee break at work. This is the type of rest we are to have in this life to keep us from getting stressed out. The "rest" in Matthew 11:28 is Anapasis. (come to Me…weary and heavy laden and I will give you rest.)

OK, I just used the "s" word—stress. Now we are getting down to where we too often live!

The Greek verb—Anapauo—is used in Matthew 11:28. Jesus tells us "*I will give you rest.*" This rest is a gift He wants to give to us. We all are to take breaks, times when we don't overextend ourselves physically or spiritually. Times when we don't get walls painted or all the projects done around our house. Times when our energy is all used up and we even take a break from praying and interceding.

These are times when we just sit in God's presence and accept His gift of rest.

If we are always too busy to spend time with God, we need to change our priorities so we do not break communion with God and become *stressed*. I would like to say I always live in that place but of course it's not true. But I do always try to. If we have learned that this rest is really a gift that God wants to give us, we need to remind ourselves often that we need to accept His rest. He created rest as a gift for us. And we want all of His gifts. Right? So we need to seek it. We need to accept it, even in the midst of much activity. We need to live in an attitude of rest. Just as we walk in the Spirit, walk also in rest.

My days are really busy but, I have seen Him help me get done what I need to do in such sovereign ways at times. I didn't always know to call it "walking in His rest" but that is really what it is. Some time ago a close friend had a physical and emotional "meltdown." She realized she had been so busy seeking God for every situation, that she forgot how to seek God for herself. And she forgot how to rest in Him.

Stress has become part of our culture, in the U.S. and around the world. Every one of us have situations in our lives that are truly stressful. I've experienced many times of trauma that were very stressful times in my life.

But as I look back at all I've experienced I see how Jesus has ministered to my soul in all my times of need. He carries burdens for us that are far too heavy for us to carry ourselves.

Jesus tells us in Matthew 11: 28-30 "*Come to me, all of you who are weary and carry heavy burdens, and I will give you rest. Take my yoke upon you. Let me teach you, because I am humble and gentle, and you will find rest for your souls. For my yoke fits perfectly, and the burden I give you is light.*"

Rest does not happen automatically. Actually it's just the opposite that seems to be more automatic. We need to seek rest, and accept it as a gift from God.

We must not focus on the obstacles in our life, because God has a destiny for every one of us. Too often, just before we reach our destiny we give up because there are so many obstacles that we've encountered along the way. We might think surely God has forgotten me. Or I've missed my destiny. Surely all these things would not have happened to me if God really cared about me.

But dear ones, God does care. You are altogether lovely in His sight. He has no anger toward you. God spent it all on Jesus as He hung on the cross taking all the punishment for our sin.

# Rest and Life's Lessons

I once asked God to tell me what I've really learned through all the things I've gone through in my life. He told me I've learned:

Utter dependence on God.

That I am nothing without Him.

It is in the secret places that He meets me.

That He cries with me, rejoices with me, but through it all He asks—Do you love Me? Will you trust my love even through this?

One day as I sat on my backyard swing thinking about my life, the lives of people in my family, and the lives of so many women I know, He spoke this prophetic word to me.

"I am with you always, ready for you to lift unto Me the devastation of your soul, the weight of your grief, the sorrow you carry in your heart. Let Me carry it for you. Empty yourself of these things that weigh you down. Give them to Me and fill yourself instead with My love. In my love you will find rest and peace. The oil of joy for mourning. Beauty for ashes."

Rest and peace. We can have that. It's for all of us.

We can allow ourselves to sit and feel the warm breeze on our face.

We can find rest in the middle of the raging battle.

We can even sit and stare at the wall sometimes when we need to just rest our mind. Get some of that Anapasis rest.

And in the deepest part of our being we can know

that rest is accepting who you are becoming in Christ. Rest is not striving for accomplishments, but relaxing in the knowledge of Christ working in you.

Rest is knowing that you are complete in Christ and that God sees who you are and who you will become. And, rest is knowing you are the fulfillment of God's hope for you in Christ.

A reporter once spoke with Martin Luther King during a long march he was leading during the civil rights days in America. He asked, "How are you doing?" Dr. King replied, "My legs are tired but there is rest in my soul."

God bless you as you seek His rest in all areas of your life.

www.ingramcontent.com/pod-product-compliance
Lightning Source LLC
Chambersburg PA
CBHW060831050426
42453CB00008B/647